Confederate Spy Stories

By Katherine and John Bakeless

Spies of the Revolution
They Saw America First

By Katherine Bakeless

Story-Lives of American Composers
Story-Lives of Great Composers

By John Bakeless

Spies of the Confederacy
Turncoats, Traitors and Heroes

Katherine and John Bakeless

Confederate Spy Stories

J. B. Lippincott Company
Philadelphia and New York

U.S. Library of Congress Cataloging in Publication Data

Bakeless, Katherine (Little) birth date
  Confederate spy stories.

  SUMMARY: Biographies of men and women who, for patriotic or mercenary reasons, engaged in espionage for the Confederacy.
  1. United States—History—Civil War—Secret service—Confederate States—Juvenile literature. [1. United States—History—Civil War—Secret service—Confederate States. 2. Spies. 3. Espionage —Biography]
I. Bakeless, John Edwin, birth date, joint author. II. Title.
E608.B14   973.7′86′0922 [B] [920]   73-4984
ISBN-0-397-31230-X

NOTE

The material in this book is based on *Spies of the Confederacy*, by John Bakeless. Copyright © 1970, by John Bakeless. Complete notes, documentation, and bibliographical references will be found there. As much of this material is nowhere else available, it can be useful to students of all ages and all levels.

Contents

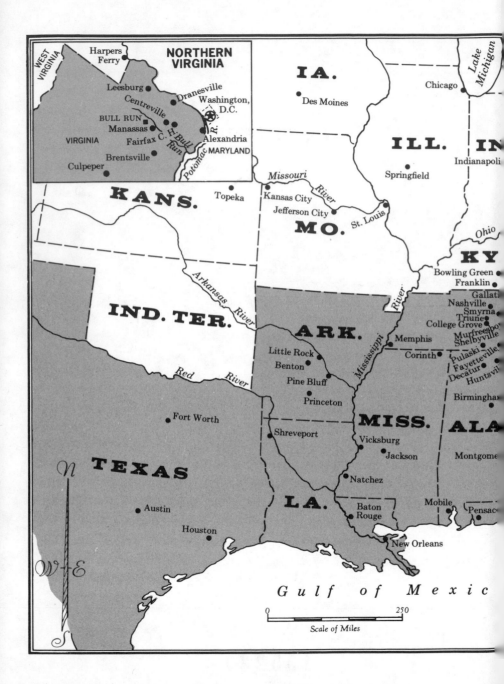

NORTHERN VIRGINIA

WEST VIRGINIA

Harpers Ferry

Leesburg

Dranesville

Centreville

Washington, D.C.

BULL RUN
Manassas

VIRGINIA

Fairfax C.H. Bull Run

Alexandria

MARYLAND

Brentsville

Culpeper

Potomac R.

IA.

Des Moines

Chicago

Lake Michigan

ILL.

IN.

Springfield

Indianapoli

KANS.

Topeka

Missouri River

Kansas City

Jefferson City

MO.

St. Louis

Ohio

KY.

Bowling Green

Franklin

Gallati

Nashville

Smyrna

Triune

College Grove

Murfreesbo

Shelbyville

Pulaski

Fayetteville

Decatur

Huntsvi

Birmingham

Arkansas River

IND. TER.

ARK.

Memphis

Corinth

Little Rock

Benton

Pine Bluff

Princeton

Red River

Fort Worth

Shreveport

MISS.

ALA.

Vicksburg

Jackson

Montgome

TEXAS

Natchez

LA.

Austin

Houston

Baton Rouge

Mobile

Pensac

New Orleans

N

W E

S

Gulf of Mexic

0   250

Scale of Miles

The Confederate States

1

Why Spy?

General Dwight D. Eisenhower once remarked: "Nothing is more important to a commander than the facts concerning the strength, dispositions, and intentions of his opponent." The general thus summed up the need for military intelligence, of which espionage is an important part.

It is usually possible to get a fairly accurate idea how many soldiers an enemy has, though it is also possible to make tremendous and sometimes fatal errors. Careful scouting and patrolling, interrogation of enemy prisoners, and, in our modern days, air observation usually give a fairly clear idea of the location of the enemy's troops.

It is, however, not often possible to be sure of the exact intentions of the enemy. That is why textbooks of military intelligence usually urge staff officers to try to list the capabilities of the enemy—in another words, what the enemy can do, rather than what they think the enemy is going to do. But, as a practical matter, no commander is satisfied merely to have his staff tell him what the enemy can do. He is practically certain to ask his intelligence officer what the enemy *will* do. In that case, the intelligence officer has to choose the most probable "capability."

How can a commander find out either enemy capabilities or enemy intentions? The enemy certainly isn't going to tell him! If a commander tries to find out for himself, the enemy will try to stop it. He will use his military police, ordinary police, detectives, counterespionage services, and any traitors there may be within the commander's own forces—men like Benedict Arnold.

A commander in the field has troops available for reconnoissance. He can send these men out as single scouts or in small groups called patrols. He can conduct what is called a "reconnoissance in force." That is, he can send out a number of troops, sometimes as large a force as a regiment or a brigade, to do a little careful fighting—not to defeat the enemy, but to force the enemy to reveal, by the nature of his resistance, what his intentions really are. A commander can also send airplanes over the enemy lines. He can listen in on the enemy's field telephones and radio. He can send out raiders to bring in prisoners for interrogation.

There comes a time, however, when these methods are not enough. They cannot reveal what is being said in the enemy's headquarters. They cannot reveal how large a store of munitions he has within his supply dumps. They cannot penetrate his War Department to find out what is being planned there.

At this point, a commander needs spies to find out the

enemy's strength, his capabilities, the location of his troops, the nature of his weapons, and his war plans. Even the personality of the enemy commander is important, for that may be a guide to what is going to happen. Is he bold or overcautious? In World War I, every Allied staff knew that if General von Mackensen appeared on their front, the Germans would attack immediately.

Because a spy can do so much damage, he suffers severely if captured. The usual penalty, under the rules of land warfare and various international treaties, is death, usually by shooting or hanging, though the United States electrocuted some German spies during World War II. A scout caught reconnoitering in uniform, however, is not punished at all. His uniform shows plainly that he is an enemy soldier, and, like any other soldier, a scout, if captured, is merely made a prisoner of war.

Many spies are patriots who risk a disgraceful death in order to do what they consider their duty to their country. One of these, Major John André, the British spy caught in civilian clothes on his way from West Point to the British forces in New York City during the American Revolution, was greatly admired by the American officers who guarded him on his last walk to execution. The court-martial that condemned him to death did so with regret.

It may seem dreadful and cruel that a brave and innocent man who has done his duty should be executed like a common criminal. But war itself is both dreadful and cruel. The death penalty is inflicted to make people hesitate to undertake espionage, and, because it is so dangerous, neither soldiers nor civilians are ever ordered to such duty. They must always volunteer.

Not all spies are patriots or heroes. There are also mercenary spies—in it for cash. They do volunteer, but they accept the dreadful risks they have to run merely for money—and in certain cases the pay for espionage is very high indeed. Some of these mercenary spies are willing to spy even upon their own countries, as Benedict Arnold did.

Men and women who run such risks solely out of loyalty to their countries ought to be honored, but they rarely are. Usually they are not even known—they work and die in secrecy. But England has placed a monument to Major André in Westminster Abbey. There are two monuments in Connecticut and one in New York to honor Nathan Hale, and a monument to Daniel Bissell, one of Washington's bravest spies, in Windsor, Connecticut, where he lived. Bissell was one of the first three Americans to receive the Purple Heart, a decoration now given only to the wounded. Nobody has built a monument to Benedict Arnold, whom both the Americans and British came to despise; but on the battlefield at Saratoga, New York, there is a monument to his leg, which was wounded at the siege of Quebec and again at Saratoga, while he was still a brave and loyal American officer.

A few technical terms connected with espionage ought to be defined. Since spies' messages must be secret, they are usually sent in cipher or code. Cipher is a special alphabet with special letters. Anyone who doesn't know the cipher alphabet can't read the message, unless he can "break" the cipher—that is, discover what each letter means. This isn't too hard to do with simple ciphers. The most common letters in written English are, in order, *e,t,a,o,i,n*. Find the letter symbol most often used and you have *e*. The next in frequency will be *t* and *a*. If a symbol frequently follows *t*, it is probably *h*, as in *this, that, those, these, the, then, them, there*—words commonly used in English. Edgar Allan Poe showed how to break such a simple cipher in his story "The Gold Bug."

Breaking a cipher can be made harder by using "nulls"—symbols that don't mean anything at all—or by using several symbols to mean *e*, several others to mean *a*, and so forth. But in the long run, all ciphers can be broken.

Code is a form of secret writing in which no alphabet is used. Each word is represented by another word, usually a meaningless jumble of letters, like *qxrwd*, or by numbers. During the American Revolution, Washington used a numerical code in which a number represented a given word. To make a code harder to break, each word may have several symbols. Code-breaking can be made harder still if the coded message is put into cipher, too. A secret message can also be typed on a special machine that turns it into code or cipher, after which another machine will turn it back into "clear."

Each time a new method of secret writing is invented, people think it is unbreakable, but, in the end, it can always be broken. In World War II, the Japanese believed their machine code, called the "Purple Code," was unbreakable, but an American Army-Navy team was soon "breaking" each message as it came. They worked so swiftly that President Roosevelt was able to read the last message to the Japanese Ambassador before Pearl Harbor, when it had not yet been decoded for the

Ambassador himself. During the Civil War, the Confederates once tapped the telegraph line between General Grant and the War Department, but they could not break the code (or cipher) Grant was using.

A few terms in military intelligence may need explanation. A double spy is one working for both sides. He may be merely pretending to work for the enemy and sincerely working for his own country, or vice versa. Civil War General Philip H. Sheridan had a star spy, entirely loyal to the Union, whom he ordered to give information to the Confederates. General Sheridan insisted it should be correct information. In that way, the spy would win the Confederates' confidence, and by giving them a little correct information, Sheridan hoped he would get a great deal of correct information for the Union. The scheme worked, too. Some double spies, however, are traitors to both sides, betraying any information they can get for the cash there is in it.

A network is a group of spies, spread over a country, or part of a country, or several countries, so that they cover their territory like a net. They make their reports and receive their instructions by couriers (secret messengers) or sometimes through the ordinary mail—as they did in the Civil War. Today they sometimes use secret radio; but that is dangerous, for their hidden sending stations can be located by the enemy's listening posts. Many of the spies in a network are resident agents—that is, they live permanently in the countries on which they are spying, become local citizens, sometimes prominent ones, and report secretly whatever they can learn.

To escape detection, spies often use letterdrops—secret

places where they can leave messages for couriers to pick up. Sometimes, for extra security, two letterdrops are used. The spy never knows who the courier is; the courier never sees the spy. In the Civil War, the Confederate secret agent, Frank Stringfellow, had a letterdrop under the eaves of the house of the dentist for whom he worked. In the morning he always found the letters he had placed there were gone, but he never knew who took them.

Counterintelligence agents are spy-catchers. The word is also sometimes used for men who try to "plant" false information so the enemy will believe it.

Guerrillas are irregular troops, often not in uniform, who fight in a secret way and sometimes are also scouts and spies. They are very dangerous and hard to handle and are liable to be executed, if caught, for being out of uniform. In the Civil War they were called bushwhackers, because they struck or "whacked" from concealment in woods and bushes.

Military organization in the Civil War was similar to that of today but the units were smaller. For example, a Union company was supposed to have 101 officers and men, a regiment between 845 and 1,025 men. Both company and regiment are nearly three times as large today. Of course, the strength of the units sank as men were killed, wounded, or captured. Since new men could not always be supplied, some units—especially in the Confederate Army, which was based on a smaller population—had almost no men when the war ended.

A brigade consisted of two or more regiments, a division of two or more brigades, and an army corps of two or more divisions. All these units are larger today because modern means of communication make it easier to send orders swiftly here and there to control the troops. In the Civil War, troops had to be controlled by orders shouted above the firing, by bugle calls, by drums, or by mounted messengers.

2

Confederate Spies in Washington

The Southern states entered the Civil War with certain marked advantages over their Northern opponents. One great advantage was that, to win the war, the Confederates had only to defend themselves. They were not trying to conquer the North; all they wanted was to get out of the Union. The Northern states, on the other hand, believed the South had no right to leave the "indissoluble" Union. In order to prevent secession, the Northern states had first to conquer the eleven Southern states, then occupy their territory.

The Confederates had the further military advantage of interior lines. They could shift troops and supplies back and forth across a relatively short distance inside the curve of the front. The North had to operate on the outside of the curve—a much longer distance.

The South had still another advantage. Their men were a hardy outdoor breed, primarily rural, accustomed to horses, firearms, and an outdoor life. Northern soldiers, largely town and city bred, often had to be taught to shoot, stay on a horse, march, camp, and live in the open.

The Southerners were also fortunate in discovering, at the very beginning of the war, a group of superb generals, three of whom—Robert E. Lee, Stonewall Jackson, and J. E. B. (Jeb) Stuart—rank among the great captains of all time. More than half the Civil War was over before President Lincoln could find commanders able to cope with them.

The Confederate states had one other and even greater advantage. They began the war with an already organized and highly efficient espionage system, with tentacles reaching into the vital secrets of the Federal government, especially the War Department. Often their spies could report what the Yankees were going to do almost as soon as the decision was reached—and before the troops in blue began to move.

The North, on the other hand, had nothing of the sort when hostilities began. After the Southern states started to secede and it was clear there would be a war, there was no way to work Yankee spies into the Confederate government, because there was no Confederate government yet. No one knew what that government would be, which states would join it, where it would have its capital, how strong its army would be, or which generals would take command.

Eventually, as hostilities went on, the Union intelligence services came to equal their Southern rivals in securing information. But they never succeeded in protecting their own secrets from the Confederate spies, who continued to work their way into the highest Federal headquarters in the field and into government offices in Washington, until the very end.

Before the war began, while the secession movement was growing, Southern sympathizers in Washington were in an ideal position for espionage. They could remain in their Washington homes and offices and spy on everything the Union government was doing. Border states like Delaware, Maryland, and Kentucky were the homes of innumerable Southern sympathizers. Younger men slipped away to join the army in gray. The women and the older men could be useful as secret agents, as messengers, and as smugglers of medical supplies, recruits, arms, uniforms, and ammunition. All this was aided by a widespread and well-organized secret society, the Knights of the Golden Circle, which had Northern and Southern branches closely co-operating with each other.

The North had few such advantages. It had no friends in high positions in Jefferson Davis's government. In fact, it was not decided until 1861 that Jefferson Davis was to be the President of the Confederacy and that the capital was to be in Richmond, Virginia. Nor could the North rely on many sympathizers in the South. Even men like Robert E. Lee—who had been a graduate and later Superintendent of West Point, and who was personally opposed to the secession of the Southern states and devoted to the Union—felt it a duty to "go with their states." It took a long time for the Northern army to find Southerners willing to risk their lives as secret agents for the Union. After that, it took still more time to organize them into a system.

To remedy this situation, one of the first things General George Brinton McClellan did when he assumed command of the Union armies was to appoint a chief of intelligence. He sent at once for the famous Chicago detective, Allan Pinkerton.

Pinkerton knew a great deal about catching criminals. During the Civil War, he showed that he also knew a great deal about catching Confederate spies. What he didn't know was how to be a spy himself, reporting on the problems of army organization, morale, strength, probable movements, weapons, and all the things an intelligence department must find out. Nor did he know how to evaluate military intelligence, that is, how to separate accurate from inaccurate information. The worst mistake he made was to overestimate Confederate strength, repeatedly telling General McClellan that the Confederate Army was many times stronger than it really was. McClellan was afraid to attack, because he believed Pinkerton's exaggerated estimates of Confederate strength; and, when he finally did muster courage enough to make an attack, he failed. In the end, McClellan had to be relieved, General John A. Pope replaced him in command, and Pinkerton went back to hunting criminals, including spies, work that he really understood.

As soon as it began to seem likely—long before the Southern states had actually seceded—that hostilities between North and South would eventually break out, various devoted Southern volunteers began to set up an elaborate Confederate secret intelligence system in Washington. They could learn everything the Federals were doing, since there were still practically no security precautions. As most of the higher Confederate civilian officials had formerly been Federal officials, they knew the operations of the Federal government from the inside. Leading Confederate Army officers, graduates of West Point, had previously been United States Army officers. They knew all about the army they were now going to fight. The Secretary of War, as late as December, 1860, was a future Confederate general.

During the months before hostilities, while the Southern states were seceding one by one, Confederate espionage in Washington operated in an almost friendly atmosphere. Army and Navy officers from the South who had resigned from the United States services and were on their way to join the Confederates were allowed to pass freely through Washington, observing anything they wished. They traveled without any restriction and they carried much valuable information south with them. The supposedly secret voyage of the Federal steamer *Star of the West*, sent by President Lincoln to supply Fort Sumter, was betrayed to the Confederates by Jacob Thompson, who had been Secretary of the Interior under President Buchanan.

When civilian officials and army and navy officers from the Southern states had all gone home, a host of Southerners still remained in Washington as private individuals. Some, though their homes were in Dixie, put loyalty to the Union above loyalty to their states   men like the Virginian commander-in-chief of the U.S. Army, General Winfield Scott, or the future "Rock of Chickamauga," General George H. Thomas, or the remarkable Federal spy "Chickasaw," who came from Alabama. But many others were intensely loyal to the South. Some were social leaders from Southern families who had lived for years in Washington. Some were minor officials, safely ensconced in Federal jobs, ideally situated for treason. Some of these agents operated throughout the war, never suspected, never discovered, never confessing, unknown even today—save for the information they transmitted. Others, outside the government, provided shelter, emergency funds, or transportation to Confederate spies.

Charming Southern ladies who had long made their homes in the nation's capital stayed in those homes and continued to charm information out of incautious Northern officers, all for the benefit of the Confederacy. Many of these women came from border states like Maryland, which never formally seceded, but in which Southern sympathies were strong. Among these Dixieland sirens, Mrs. Rose O'Neal Greenhow—an astute and wealthy hostess of fanatically Southern sympathies—was "reputed to be the most persuasive woman that was ever known in Washington." The "Rebel Rose" was head of the first Confederate spy net established in the capital.

Southern espionage entered the Presidential family circle in the White House itself. Shortly after Lincoln's inauguration, Mrs. Lincoln, a Kentuckian with a brother, three half-brothers, and three brothers-in-law in the Confederate Army, found that one of her White House guests was "in the habit of listening about the Cabinet room doors" and then "retailing all the information he could thus gather to those only too willing to make use of it." When President Lincoln gave his sister-in-law a pass to go through the lines, the lady carried south "her weight, almost, in quinine," a medicine the Confederates badly needed and were desperately trying to get.

Such incidents make it easy to believe the statement, sometimes made, that every decision of Lincoln's cabinet during the first months of the war was known in Richmond within twenty-four hours. Many other leaks were due to other individuals like Mrs. Lincoln's eavesdropping guest, to careless talk, and to numerous disloyal postmasters in Maryland towns who helped speed treasonable messages on their way and probably supplied a good deal of secret information themselves.

At least three Confederate spy rings existed in Washington at various periods of the Civil War. The first was directed by Mrs. Greenhow; the second by Captain Thomas Nelson Conrad, chaplain of the 3rd Virginia Cavalry, who doubled as an amazingly successful intelligence officer, operating for General Jeb Stuart; and a third system, set up late in the war, by Frank Stringfellow, 4th Virginia Cavalry, another of Stuart's star secret agents.

It is doubtful if any of these spy rings were connected. Both Mrs. Greenhow and Captain Conrad later published accounts of their adventures, but neither mentions the other, though both are surprisingly frank. They do not seem to have known any more about Stringfellow than he knew about them.

There were also many Confederate sympathizers connected with no networks at all, who gathered up such information as they could find in Washington and the Army's outpost lines along the Potomac River, sending it on to Confederate intelligence officers by methods of their own devising. One learns about them mostly from records of arrest and trial, or from reports of indignant pro-Union informants. But about the really clever ones, too clever to attract attention, the rest is silence.

3

The Rebel Rose

Captain Thomas Jordan, U.S. Army, established the first Confederate spy net—which he eventually turned over to Mrs. Greenhow's management—sometime late in 1860 or perhaps early in 1861. Under Mrs. Greenhow's management, the ring worked undisturbed until August, 1861, when she and some of her best spies were arrested and the spy ring was broken up.

Jordan had graduated from West Point and had made a good record in the Seminole Indian Wars and in the Mexican War. When hostilities ended in Mexico, he had helped plan the homeward movement of General Winfield Scott's troops. Now, in 1860–1861, as the states began to secede, Scott, though a Virginian, was General-in-Chief of the Army, and so in charge of Northern war plans. Captain Jordan must have found his association with General Scott a great help in his Confederate espionage—of which the general knew nothing. By the time Jordan did resign from the Union Army, he had organized Confederate espionage in Washington so well that Mrs. Greenhow could carry on. She continued to receive reports from the various spies who had previously worked for Captain Jordan. She could send their information on in cipher through a secret courier system running directly to the Confederate headquarters of General Beauregard, where Jordan was now a staff officer, and thence on to Richmond.

Captain Jordan could not have found a better leader for his spy ring than Mrs. Greenhow. Born in Maryland, she had grown up as a "pampered Washington belle" in the capital's political atmosphere. She was an ardent secessionist. Widely acquainted in government circles since girlhood, she had acquired a surprising degree of influence, which she was very willing to use in the service of the Confederates.

Allan Pinkerton, the detective, reported that Mrs. Greenhow had "secret and insidious agents in all parts of this city [i.e., Washington] and scattered over a large extent of country." This last statement explains why papers written in the ciphers used by the Rebel Rose eventually turned up hundreds of miles from the capital.

Before the death of her husband, Dr. Robert Greenhow, a State Department official, Mrs. Greenhow had become well acquainted with other State Department officials and with many of the foreign diplomats stationed in Washington. After Dr. Greenhow's death, his wealthy widow continued to live there and became a recognized power in a city where petticoat influence has always been powerful. The political pull she had long possessed increased during President James Buchanan's administration, for Mrs. Greenhow and the bachelor President had long been close friends, corresponding on political affairs, even while Buchanan was abroad as Minister to the Court of St. James's. After he became President, Buchanan continued to call on Mrs. Greenhow frequently, in spite of the tradition that the President of the United States does not call at private homes.

Her list of friends and admirers in high places in the Federal government was indeed impressive. The Secretary of State, William H. Seward, dined at her beautifully appointed table, along with other officials and equally distinguished guests. The lady's most ardent admirer was Senator Henry Wilson of Massachusetts, then chairman of the Senate Military Affairs Committee, a good man for a Confederate spy to know.

Senator Wilson's flaming love letters to her, which he signed with an "H," were written on Senate stationery! They were seized when Mrs. Greenhow was arrested and are now in the National Archives. One letter says, "You well know that I love you—and will sacrifice anything," but he fears he will bring her into trouble. "You know that I *do love* you," he goes on. "I am suffering this morning, in fact I am sick physically and mentally, and know that nothing would soothe me so much as an hour with you. I will be with you tonight, and then I will tell you again and again that I love you." The ardor of these letters suggests that Mrs. Greenhow had no difficulty in wheedling whatever information she wanted from this particular admirer.

After the war was over, Jordan admitted that he was partly responsible for this. He had learned of an "intimacy" between the charming widow and the susceptible senator. After he knew about it, he himself cultivated her acquaintance and then "induced her to get from Wilson all the information she could."

From the senator, Mrs. Greenhow learned what General Scott was writing to Senator Wilson. She learned what General McClellan had said to Senator Wilson when they conversed in President Lincoln's reception room in the White House. "She knew my plans," McClellan wrote, "and has four times compelled me to change them." She learned McClellan's scheme for army reorganization, which should never have gone beyond the inner circles of the War Department. She learned useful facts about the U.S. Navy's strength and plans.

Soldiers as well as politicians and government clerks were useful to her. Rebel Rose's artful wiles caused one disgusted Federal to complain (much too late, when the truth began to come out): "She has not used her powers in vain among the officers of the army, not a few of whom she has robbed of patriotic hearts."

All this time, through her agents and couriers, she was in almost daily contact with General Beauregard's headquarters, where Jordan had gone. All Mrs. Greenhow's information went flying on to Jordan, who could give it to General Beauregard or forward it. It is no wonder General Beauregard said later he was as well informed on affairs in Washington as the United States officials working there.

4

The Spies Who Won
Bull Run

The two remarkable Confederate triumphs with which the Civil War began—the capture of the Harpers Ferry arsenal and the victory at Bull Run—were both the results of early and correct military intelligence and of the speed with which the Confederate leaders recognized the accuracy of the information and acted upon it.

By a queer sort of irony, however, the seizure of Harpers Ferry (April 18, 1861) with several million dollars' worth of ordnance supplies had no connection whatever with the elaborate intelligence network Captain Jordan and Mrs. Greenhow had labored so assiduously to establish. This was especially odd because Captain Jordan, still on duty at the War Department, should have known for months that this important post had a garrison of the men in blue so small that they could not possibly defend it.

As Virginia approached secession, which could easily be foreseen by April 15, 1861, the U.S. Army prepared to strengthen this little garrison. Curiously, no word of warning from Captain Jordan or the Rebel Rose reached the Southern leaders. The Confederates would not have captured the arsenal at all—not in 1861, at least—had it not been for the swift intervention of two Confederate volunteer spies, both complete amateurs, who had no connection with any networks.

Lieutenant Roger Jones, a U.S. Regular, guarded Harpers Ferry with a small detachment of forty-eight soldiers. They had been sent there in January when the superintendent warned Washington the arsenal was in danger of attack. As mid-April drew near and Virginia's secession seemed more and more likely, Lieutenant Jones, who knew his little guard was totally inadequate, sent a secret messenger to Washington, asking for reinforcements. But the messenger lost courage and simply went home.

The Confederates already had a force of Virginia militia standing by, ready to seize the arsenal as soon as their state formally left the Union. Captain John Imboden, who later became a Confederate general, loaded ammunition on a passenger train, put some Virginia state troops aboard, and started off to seize the arsenal before Union reinforcements could arrive. Just before the train pulled out, a Confederate soldier's careless remark roused the suspicion of a Northern passenger. This Yankee immediately wrote out a telegraphic warning to President Lincoln but, as the train was ready to start, could not send it himself. He gave it to a Negro with instructions to take it to the nearest telegraph office and handed him a dollar, a good deal of money in those days.

If that telegram had ever reached Washington, Harpers Ferry might have been reinforced in time, and the arsenal saved to equip the Union forces. But an equally observant Southern passenger had noticed what the Yankee was doing. He could not leave the train either, but he sent a friend to follow the Negro, stop him, and take away the message before he could reach the telegraph office.

No Union forces ever reached Harpers Ferry to help Lieutenant Jones and his forty-eight men, though there was an attempt to save them.

This was made by the driver of the locomotive pulling the train on which the Virginia troops were traveling, who was a Union sympathizer. Northern engineers were common in the South because skill with machinery was rare in the cotton states, where agricultural pursuits were paramount. Many a clever Yankee mechanic went south to drive railroad engines. The man at the throttle of the locomotive on April 17 was one of these, and he could easily guess the mission of the armed men traveling in the cars behind his engine. To delay the militiamen, this engineer let his fires go out, as if by accident, and the train came to a stop. But the Confederates forced him at pistol point to fire up again and run the train on, with no great loss of time.

At Harpers Ferry, Lieutenant Jones, seeing his danger, set fire to the arsenal, destroying between seventeen thousand and twenty thousand small arms, which both Union and Confederate armies badly needed. What the Union thus lost, the Confederates did not win, but they were now in possession of Harpers Ferry and much of the arsenal's machinery.

This achievement was followed in July by the overwhelming Confederate victory at Bull Run, made possible by the essential information supplied to the Confederates by the Jordan-Greenhow organization. Though this particular spy net did not last long, its success at Bull Run fully justified all the work and danger the espionage required.

General Beauregard soon found that he and his Confederate officers could trust the "arrangements" made "through the foresight of Colonel Thomas Jordan." After the war, he said that Jordan's "arrangements" enabled him "to receive regularly, from private persons at the Federal capital, most accurate information." After this information was collected, it was sent south by Mrs. Rose Greenhow. Though she had been supplying intelligence months before Bull Run and continued to supply it for some time afterward, her greatest service of the entire war was the information she sent before that battle. This told Beauregard exactly what Federal General McDowell was going to do, long before McDowell had a chance to do it.

On July 4, 1861, a little more than two weeks before the battle, Beauregard secured additional authentic information from other sources, confirming the reports he had already received. The most important confirmation came when, by a great stroke of luck, his outposts caught a Union soldier who had been on duty in the Washington office of the U.S. Army's adjutant general, compiling strength returns to about July 1. The prisoner was willing to talk.

Prisoners or deserters eager to provide intelligence about their own army have to be handled with care. They may be sincere, but they may also be enemy "plants," sent to give deceptive false information. Using such plants was a favorite Confederate trick, as it was with the Federals. Since one great aim in espionage is to supply the enemy with the wrong information, the receiver of intelligence must always be on guard against deceit.

This man, however, seemed to be genuine, though it was suspicious that an enlisted man from enemy head-quarters should be found at the front, so near the Confederate outposts. But this prisoner's figures on General McDowell's strength tallied so closely with those sent from Washington (Rebel Rose through Jordan) that Beauregard felt sure they were accurate. Further confirmation of these Union strength reports was sup-plied by Northern newspapers, which were regularly and secretly sent to the Confederate general from the Federal capital. The Federals had been unable to stop them.

Though Beauregard thus knew what Union strength was and where Union forces were, he still had to find out what General McDowell was going to do with them. Thanks to his Washington spies, Beauregard was lucky enough to learn in advance exactly what General McDowell meant to do, and the very day when he was going to do it. The Rebel Rose supplied this precious information in not one, but *three* messages, which were sent July 10, 16, and 17.

General McDowell had very little choice. He had to march south and attack Beauregard's Confederates at Bull Run. Otherwise, most of his army would go home without having done anything at all, for his men's enlistments were running out. President Lincoln had issued a call for three-month volunteers, though most of these men could not be mustered into service until some weeks later. By mid-July, these enlistments were beginning to expire. Some Union troops actually marched away and left the Bull Run battlefield, at the very moment when they were needed most, because their time was up.

Beauregard wanted the Yankees to attack him. He had a good defensive position at Manassas, close to his bases but far enough north to defend Virginia, and with General Joseph E. Johnston's army in the Shenandoah Valley close enough to give him support. That is why he wrote to Richmond: "If I could only get the enemy to attack me, as I am trying to have him do, I would stake my reputation on the handsomest victory that could be hoped for."

If General Beauregard wanted General McDowell to attack him, he was going to get his wish. Mrs. Greenhow's messages told him General McDowell was preparing to do exactly that.

Her messenger was Betty Duvall, the young and pretty daughter of a Maryland couple who were living in Washington. Betty knew the country and the people on both sides of the Potomac River and, like most Southern girls of the period, was experienced with horses. After enciphering the message to Beauregard, Mrs. Greenhow folded it into a tiny packet, which she sewed up in a bit of silk. This she fastened into Betty's luxuriant black hair, where it was held in place by a "tucking comb," a rather large, curved, and often fancy comb stuck in the back of the head to hold up a large coil of long hair. The Confederates had evidently used this method of concealment before. Another lady's *Diary from Dixie*, in an entry of July 13, a few days earlier, refers to spies "from

Washington, galloping in with the exact number of the enemy done up in their hair."

Very plainly dressed to look like a farmer's daughter, Betty boldly drove an ordinary farm cart out of Washington and across the Potomac over the Chain Bridge about noon on July 10, 1861. The city of Washington was in a turmoil that day, and everybody could see what was going to happen. It is impossible to conceal preparations for the movement of a large force. Mrs. Greenhow herself described the conditions that gave away the secret: "Officers and orderlies on horse were seen flying from place to place; the tramp of armed men was heard on every side—martial music filled the air." Field trains were being prepared. Transport and combat wagons were being loaded. Confederate spies merely had to stroll about the streets to see that an advance was imminent. Nobody bothered about a young country girl driving a farm cart out of the city.

Betty stopped for the night at the Virginia home of Lieutenant Catesby Jones, who had been in the U.S. Navy but was now an officer in the new Confederate Navy. In the morning she looked different. Now she was dressed in a smart riding habit and, with her girl cousin for a companion, rode toward Fairfax Court House. Somewhere near there a Confederate picket stopped her. She had run into General Bonham's outpost lines, and the pickets had been given orders that no more women were to pass. The general seems to have suspected that Yankee female spies were slipping through.

After some argument, Betty persuaded the suspicious soldier to send her on. She said she knew General

Bonham, or rather he knew her and would be glad to see
her. She won, and the provost marshal himself conducted
her to the general. General Bonham's report of this
occasion says that the provost marshal brought to him "a
beautiful young lady, a brunette with sparkling black
eyes, perfect features, glossy black hair." She was "of
medium height," and he could see "the glow of patriotic
devotion burning in her face."

Betty told the general that she had important information for General Beauregard. Could she have permission
to take it on to him at once? If not, would General
Bonham forward it immediately?

Bonham replied that he "would have it faithfully
forwarded at once."

Thus assured, Betty "took out her tucking comb and
let fall the longest and most beautiful roll of hair that I
have ever seen." She then, he reported, took "from the
back of her head, where it had been safely tied, a small
package, not larger than a silver dollar, sewed up in silk."
Bonham rushed the little packet off to General Beauregard, who later sent it by officer courier to President
Jefferson Davis. The message said: "McDowell has
certainly been ordered to advance on the sixteenth.
R.O.G."

Events soon proved Mrs. Greenhow's complete accuracy. General McDowell's troops did begin to move
toward Bull Run on July 16, as she had predicted. But
Beauregard's army, warned by her, was ready and
waiting in position, with a line of outguards well forward,
beyond the stream.

As McDowell continued his preparations, with forces
larger than those of the waiting Confederates, the

situation grew tense. Beauregard needed more information from sources inside Washington.

Lieutenant Colonel Jordan made arrangements. Presently, a quiet civilian traveler appeared on the southern bank of the Potomac and crossed in a boat—which just happened to be right where he needed it. It was rowed by an oarsman—who also just happened to be in the right place at the right moment. On the other side the traveler secured a horse and buggy with no trouble at all, and drove to Washington. Everything "clicked"—all quite easy when Jordan made "arrangements!"

The silent traveler was George Donellan, a surveyor and engineer who had been an official in the Land Office until Lincoln's inauguration, when he resigned. This man arrived at Mrs. Greenhow's home on Sixteenth Street in the early morning of July 16. The maid who received him roused the sleeping Mrs. Greenhow. Either she had not known Donellan when he was in the Department of the Interior, or else she thought it wise to pretend that he was a stranger.

Who had sent him?

"Mr. Rayford, of Virginia."

Thomas J. Rayford was the pseudonym Lieutenant Colonel Jordan used for his intelligence work. But anyone could say that, and she asked for further identification. Donellan handed over a cipher message which said, "Trust bearer."

This was enough. The Rebel Rose gave the courier Donellan the second of her three vital messages. This gave the number of McDowell's troops and the route he was taking.

Donellan left Washington with the message and

reached Beauregard's camp at eight o'clock that night. By that time the Confederate pickets had already been pushed back, and the courier had to force his way past the advancing Yankee columns. But nobody stopped him. McDowell's half-trained officers never thought of halting an unexplained civilian, even though he was riding straight toward the enemy!

The speed of the Confederates' communication system is surprising. By noon of the seventeenth, Mrs. Greenhow had an answer from Jordan: "Yours was received at eight o'clock at night. Let them come; we are ready for them. We rely upon you for precise information. Be particular as to description and destination of forces, quantity of artillery, etc."

That very night, on the seventeenth, Mrs. Greenhow sent her third message. She had just learned that the Federals hoped to cut the railroad between Winchester and Manassas, in order to delay General Johnston's Confederates moving from the Shenandoah Valley to reinforce Beauregard at Manassas. But the Federals never succeeded in doing this, no doubt because of the lady spy's secret warning. The Federals would almost certainly have won at Bull Run if they had cut that railroad, for it was the sudden arrival of Johnston's army that gave the Confederates the victory.

Though the High Command in Richmond had learned to trust Mrs. Greenhow, General Beauregard was glad to have two separate confirmations of her reports. One was an intelligence report from a spy with a glass eye named John Burke who, though a Texan in a Texas regiment, had been born in the North and thus possessed a Northern accent which enabled him to talk with

Yankees without arousing suspicion. The other confirmation was brought by a pretty blonde named Antonia Ford, the daughter of a merchant of Fairfax Court House, Virginia. The Ford home was situated midway between Washington and Manassas, so that the whole Ford family could watch McDowell's troops marching south and tell what roads they were taking.

On July 19, three days after Mrs. Greenhow's first crucial report and two days before the battle, Antonia appeared at Beauregard's camp. She had walked six miles from her father's house to her grandfather's, had secured a horse there, and had persuaded an aunt to go with her to warn the general.

Antonia Ford's news of the Federal advance was welcome confirmation of Mrs. Greenhow's earlier reports. But the Confederate staff officers, who knew nothing about Antonia, were at first suspicious. Was she a genuine Confederate sympathizer? The girl might be a Federal plant. Giving the enemy a few accurate facts that they are sure to discover anyway is an old, old game; every double agent in history has used it to make his false information seem genuine.

On general principles, Beauregard's staff arrested Antonia and sent her under guard to Brentsville, a small town south of Manassas, lest she carry information back to the Union forces. But about this time, John Burke turned up with further confirmation. Before long, events also confirmed the accuracy of the information, and Antonia was released after twenty-four hours. She had to return home by a circuitous route, for the roads were now swarming with bluecoats.

The Confederate High Command had sent General

Joseph Johnston into the Shenandoah Valley to contain Patterson's much larger Union forces. But Johnston received new orders after midnight on July 18, 1861, only a few hours after Mrs. Greenhow had sent her third message. He was now to move to Manassas to support Beauregard. His problem was how to keep Patterson where he was, so that he would not go to join McDowell or attack Johnston on the march.

Johnston had under him two officers of no reputation —as yet. One was Thomas Jonathan Jackson, a brigade commander who would soon be known as Stonewall Jackson; the other a young cavalry officer named J. E. B. Stuart, who was to become the most renowned cavalry officer in either army. Colonel Jeb Stuart managed to bluff Patterson into staying where he was, holding back Patterson's eighteen thousand men with one regiment, after which he followed Johnston to Manassas.

Patterson, with his larger force, could easily have pursued Johnston and forced him to give battle, thus delaying his joining Beauregard or preventing it entirely, But he did not move, refusing to believe the timely reports on Confederate movements that were brought to him. He did not even send those reports to Washington. Only a few days later, the elderly General Patterson was "excused" from the Army. He was a civilian again.

5

The Greenhow Spy Ring after Bull Run

July 20, 1861, the day before the battle of Bull Run, was a day with whose events Mrs. Greenhow and the Washington spies had no concern. They had done their part of the work. The soldiers would have to finish it.

Mrs. Greenhow started for New York on the twentieth and spent the next day, while the battle was raging in Virginia, putting her second daughter, Leila, aboard ship for California, where she was to live in safety with her older sister until the war was over. The mother could see that the next few years would be stormy ones for her. Two daughters would be away from the fighting, but she could not send away her youngest, Rose, who was still a child.

In New York, Mrs. Greenhow heard the first false rumors of a Federal victory at Bull Run. Then came the later and accurate reports of a crushing Federal defeat, and she watched the ensuing panic in the streets of New York with great satisfaction.

Back in Washington on the twenty-third, Mrs. Greenhow received a message from her friend Jordan at

Manassas, which read, "Our President and our General direct me to thank you. We rely on your further information. The Confederacy owes you a debt."

She now began to consider the question of further information. Her ring of spies required many members. George Donellan, of the U.S. Land Office, managed communications, with help from Colonel Michael Thompson, a Washington lawyer whose code name was "Colonel Empty," from his initials. A well-known Washington dentist, Dr. Aaron Van Camp, carried messages and probably did espionage of his own. Colonel Thompson's clerk, Lewis McArthur, assisted with cipher. William Smithson, a banker, was in touch with the Rebel Rose and the Confederate War Department. Betty Duvall, Mrs. Bessie Hassler, and Lily Mackall were among her couriers. Various younger men had some kind of relationship with the ring. A man named Samuel Applegate may have been a double agent from the beginning, working for both sides. These were the secret eyes and ears in Washington for the Confederate headquarters in Richmond.

The same people could not be used too often as couriers, or watchful enemy eyes would become suspicious. Yet communications had to be kept moving between the Confederates spying in Washington and the Confederate headquarters in Richmond. The communications manager, Donellan, in Washington, set up his new courier line so skillfully that many of its couriers and letterdrops escaped Federal detection throughout the war. The new men he chose were devoted, skillful, and discreet. On the day of the battle at Bull Run, he sent his instructions for service as a courier in the new line to a doctor named Wyvill, or Wivill, or Whyvill, who lived near the Washington Navy Yard.

Several doctors were used, and this was the beginning of the highly effective "Doctor's Line," which continued long after Mrs. Greenhow had been arrested and her spy ring broken up. Medical men could go anywhere at any hour without arousing suspicion. Moreover, as every doctor of that day was a kind of traveling drugstore, carrying his medicines with him, his bulging pockets and large black bags excited no suspicion. A physician then paid professional calls at patients' homes either on horseback or in a buggy. It was easy for him to carry messages to a "safe house" along the southern limit of his ordinary rural practice. There another doctor would pick them up and take them farther south to another "safe house." This continued until the messages were far enough south for official Confederate secret service men to pick them up.

The Confederate victory at Bull Run was so over-whelming that obviously the next step for the victors was the capture of Washington. On the night after the battle, Stonewall Jackson declared that he could take the Federal capital with ten thousand men. Beauregard, who had a good many more men than that, was not so sure; but he submitted to President Jefferson Davis a "full plan of campaign for concentrating our forces, crushing successively McDowell and Patterson and capturing Washington."

The spies' next great task was preparation for the move. Mrs. Greenhow knew the questions Beauregard would need answers to: What was the Federal system of alarm signals? What fortifications existed? Where? How strong? How fully manned? Where emplaced? Troop movements? The incredible indifference to security in Washington was as bad as ever. All Mrs. Greenhow had to do was to have a friendly chat with the officer in charge of these matters—whom, of course, she knew!

Intelligence reports of the Greenhow ring of this period now exist only in ciphered documents which were torn to bits before the Federal detectives found them. Some of these were then pasted together, deciphered, and copied out in clear by Federal officials after the Confederate cipher had been broken. Others are still only torn scraps of paper. All these reports are now in the National Archives in Washington.

Besides preparing for the capture of Washington, Mrs. Greenhow's spies reported on the shortage of army blankets, the guards at the approaches to Washington, the railroad to Baltimore, artillery, McClellan's efforts to make his secret service more efficient, and the works in the vicinity of Washington, with a list of forts. The spies had been especially careful to study troop movements.

This kind of thing could not go on indefinitely without increasing the suspicions that had long existed, especially as Mrs. Greenhow had been much too outspoken from the very beginning. Many other Southern ladies were just as indiscreet. To make matters worse, other amateur lady spies in Washington could not avoid boasting of their share in the South's victory.

One Federal agent reported exactly what was happening: "Fine ladies were secretly giving information to the enemy." He added: "It was openly boasted that the secret information given to the rebel generals had been mainly the cause of the defeat of our armies at Bull

Run." This was the literal truth. Finally the War Department began to wake up. It became convinced that Mrs. Greenhow's espionage had to stop.

The man who eventually ended the dangerous lady's career in espionage was Allan Pinkerton. About midsummer of 1861, the famous detective received orders that a strict watch should be kept on Mrs. Greenhow's house, and that every person visiting there should be shadowed.

It was not long until Mrs. Greenhow began to notice that queer things were happening. She had suddenly ceased to hear from one of her "friends." She became aware that she was being followed. But even so, she continued to be very indiscreet. She and her friend Lily Mackall thought it rather amusing to be followed. They could not always resist the temptation to have a little fun. They liked to turn suddenly in the street, and if some one else turned, too, they followed the man they thought had been following them. But though this game may have been amusing for a time, it warned the Federals that Mrs. Greenhow was aware of the surveillance and would certainly do something to thwart them.

They would now have to take definite steps.

6

The Rebel Rose in Jail

Pinkerton had had orders to move cautiously; Mrs. Greenhow had friends in Congress. But by late August, 1861, the detective was ready to strike. It was a little more than a month since the South's victory at Bull Run. Pinkerton operatives had watched a steady stream of Confederate sympathizers, spies, and couriers knocking at Mrs. Greenhow's door. If she had had more experience in intelligence work, she would never have allowed this to take place but would have arranged less obvious ways of making contact with her couriers and agents.

After months of success, the lady was growing overbold. About this time she had had a chat with the youthful Mrs. Robert Hunt Morris. Mrs. Morris's husband was in the State Department, but she also had a brother-in-law on Beauregard's staff. Mrs. Greenhow offered to transmit a letter from Mrs. Morris to her sister, the wife of the staff officer. "I'm a personal friend of Beauregard," she said, "and if you will bring me a letter, I will see that your sister receives it."

Mrs. Morris reported this to her husband. He told her to drop the whole thing instantly and entirely.

On August 23, Mrs. Greenhow went for a "promenade" with a "diplomat," not otherwise identified. People do not usually take a promenade merely for pleasure in the subtropical heat of a Washington August, but a long walk is the safest way to make sure your conversation is not overheard. Mrs. Greenhow probably acquired a few facts from her diplomatic friend, perhaps also the "very important note" which she certainly had in her possession a little while later.

As she approached her home, she paused to inquire about a neighbor's children and managed to pick up "some valuable information" from one of her agents, who had apparently been loitering there in the hope of seeing her. Either this agent or one of the neighbors now warned her that her house had been watched all night and that she had been followed on her walk—though she probably knew that already.

The two men who had been following her were still lingering near by. She had at times been able to spot other Pinkerton operatives, but this pair she now noticed for the first time. Trying to look innocent, they walked past her house. When they reached the corner, they stopped and stood there, watching her.

When she saw that the men intended to hang about, Mrs. Greenhow guessed what was coming. She had to think fast, but fortune favored her. Just then one of her own spies came by. Pretending not to notice the watchers, she muttered to her agent as he passed, "Those men will probably arrest me. Wait at Corcoran's Corner, and see. If I raise my handkerchief to my face, give information."

The agent went whistling down the street. Rose slipped her "very important note" into her mouth, chewed it up, and swallowed it.

Having thus disposed of the incriminating message, she crossed the street and started up her front steps. Before she could get her door open, the detectives were behind her. One was Pinkerton himself, in a major's uniform.

"Is this Mrs. Greenhow?"

"Yes," she answered.

They hesitated a moment—and who can blame them? They were about to arrest a lady who was an important hostess in Washington and who had friends in the highest places.

Seeing their hesitation, Rose grew bolder and demanded, "Who are you, and what do you want?"

"We have come to arrest you," Pinkerton replied.

"By what authority?"

"By sufficient authority."

"Let me see your warrant."

This was awkward. They had no warrant. Pinkerton could only say he had oral authority from both State and War Departments.

Rose raised her handkerchief to her lips and looked to see if the watcher on the corner had understood her signal. The detectives closed in on her, one on each side; and, thus guarded, Mrs. Greenhow entered.

"I have no power to resist you," she said to her captors, "but had I been inside of my house, I would have killed one of you before I had submitted to this illegal process."

"We only obey orders."

Other Pinkerton operatives now arrived and she asked what they were going to do.

"To search," replied Pinkerton briefly.

The counterintelligence men examined the beds, drawers, wardrobes, soiled laundry, harmless papers that had been stored for years, children's scribblings, books, scraps of paper, fragments in the fireplaces, and a stove. Though Mrs. Greenhow, in the book she later wrote about her adventures as a spy, sneered at all this searching, the detectives did turn up a great deal of incriminating material, which is now preserved in the National Archives.

Pinkerton had been careful to leave no visible guard outside the house, lest he alarm other members of the spy ring who might be calling on Rose during the day. He hoped people on the street had noticed nothing unusual. He did not know about the rebel agent who had watched to see if Mrs. Greenhow signaled with her handkerchief. He hoped, of course, that he could gather in some of her agents.

But her little girl, Rose, spoiled everything for Pinkerton. She slipped outdoors and began chanting, "Mother's been arrested! Mother's been arrested!" Detectives dashed out to silence the child, but she was too quick for them and climbed a tree before they could reach her. She continued her chant from the tree until she was hauled down.

The arrest took place about eleven in the morning, and the news spread quickly. No Confederate agents appeared at the house until about three in the afternoon. Then Lily Mackall and her sister arrived. They knew they were walking into a hornet's nest, but they wanted to find out what was being done with their friend. They were held, with other visitors who came later, until about three thirty in the morning, when they were taken home under guard.

For several days, the detectives ransacked the house. Mrs. Greenhow knew that she had dangerous documents and other papers which they would find eventually if she could not manage to destroy them first. She had, for example, the cipher key that Colonel Jordan had made for her, and also a code.

Her cipher was, of course, just a secret alphabet, but her code is still interesting. For instance, "Aunt Sally" (a pseudonym actually used) was no one's real Aunt Sally, but one of the important spies. One of Mrs. Greenhow's messages told "Aunt Sally" that she had "some old shoes for *the children*." She wanted "Aunt Sally" to send "some one *down town* to take them." Decoded, "old shoes" meant "important information." "Down town" meant "across the Potomac River." "Some one" was a courier.

The Federals never found Mrs. Greenhow's copy of the cipher key, though she later took it to prison with her, used it even there for a time, and destroyed it only after she had received authority to do so from Jefferson Davis himself. Little Rose probably helped smuggle her mother's last ciphered reports from the prison, when allowed to go out to play. The inexperienced Union cryptanalysts probably had a good deal of trouble breaking the Jordan-Greenhow cipher, but in the long run they managed it.

The detectives made a rich haul of material from the

stove, into which Mrs. Greenhow had thrown a mass of documents she had torn to bits but failed to burn, and the fragments they saved are still in the National Archives in Washington.

Mrs. Greenhow was held under house arrest for some months, but her friend, Lily Mackall, soon moved in to live through the ordeal with her. Lily was allowed to come and go as she pleased. It was fairly obvious that the government men hoped she would lead them to other members of the Greenhow group. But Lily could see that, too. No one knows what precautions she took, but her shadows trailed her in vain. Even when a government agent escorted Lily to her home, important documents went along, inside Lily's shoes.

On January 18, 1862, at two in the afternoon, Mrs. Greenhow was told she was being moved and was given two hours to get ready. By four o'clock, she was in a carriage with a military guard, on her way to the Old Capitol Prison, where a room was provided for her and her little girl.

The Old Capitol Prison was filling up with prisoners, and in June, 1862, wanting to get rid of some of its prison population, the government released Mrs. Greenhow. She was taken to Fortress Monroe, where she signed a promise "not to return north of the Potomac River during the present hostilities without the permission of the Secretary of War of the U.S." Then she was sent on to Richmond. She was never to see Washington again.

On June 13, President Jefferson Davis reported in a letter from Richmond to his wife that he had seen Mrs.

Greenhow. "Madam looks much changed, and has the air of one whose nerves are shaken by mental torture."

But imprisoning Mrs. Greenhow and some of her assistants did not end Confederate intelligence work in Washington, though gravely hampering it. Important information from Washington continued to reach the Confederates. Antonia Ford and Betty Duvall were still busily spying for the South in or near the city, and presently other Confederate spy masters came into the Federal capital.

Life flowed on that summer in Richmond more or less as it had in the early days of the war in Washington. There were campfires, parades, picnics, military balls, formal receptions, war weddings, and war funerals. There were dances at the camps. The warm summer nights were fragrant with the scent of magnolia. Mothers and daughters spent their lonely days making things for the soldiers: sewing battle flags; tenting, which meant the handling of heavy cloth; making shirts; knitting socks and gloves, while they worried over their sons, husbands, fiancés, and relatives. When the North blockaded the Southern coastline, foodstuffs and materials diminished and became ever more expensive, and the South grew poorer and poorer.

Aside from sewing for the soldiers and speculating in cotton and tobacco, Mrs. Greenhow was preparing her prison diary for publication.

In early August, 1863, she sailed from Wilmington, North Carolina, to Europe, for three good reasons: she wished to get her book published in England; she wished to be with her eldest daughter, Florence, who was already in Paris; and she wanted to get her little Rose away from the life of wartime America and place her in a convent in Paris. She also hoped to propagandize for the Confederacy.

All this she accomplished. She also enjoyed life again, with her elder daughter by her side. In London, especially after publication of her book, she received great personal acclaim. She enjoyed a brilliant social life and was received by Queen Victoria. In France, she was received at the Emperor's court. She became part of the fashionable and literary circles of London, and almost persuaded Thomas Carlyle to write an article favoring the South. Her book, *My Imprisonment*, sold well in London, and she made some money. Colonel William E. Doster, whose prisoner she had been, paid sixteen dollars in gold to import a copy—he wanted to see what she had to say about the Old Capitol Prison. Everywhere and always she propagandized for her beloved South.

In 1864, a year after her arrival in England, she planned to run the blockade and return to America. She was in charge of a bag of Confederate official mail, which was to go straight to Richmond. She also had English gold coin worth three thousand dollars, some of which was in a leather bag with a cord around her neck, and some of which was sewn into her clothing.

The blockade-runner on which she was traveling reached the coast near Wilmington, North Carolina, safely; but, as the ship crept up the Cape Fear River, the officer on duty mistook a wrecked ship, lying in the water, for a Federal man-of-war. He swung his own helm round—and grounded his ship. At this moment his crew saw a real Federal warship coming up behind them.

It was no place for Mrs. Greenhow. Though warned of danger, she demanded to be put ashore in a small boat with some other Confederate agents. The boat overturned in the storm and the weight of the gold dragged her down. Her body was found on the beach next morning, with the bag of gold still around her neck.

7

J. E. B. Stuart's Spy, Captain Conrad

The arrest of Mrs. Greenhow in August, 1861, the discovery of so many of her agents, and her deportation broke up her espionage ring. But destroying her organization did the Union cause little good since it was replaced by two others, equally efficient and conducted with such skill that both were able to operate undiscovered throughout the rest of the war.

These two formidable spy rings operated mostly for Jeb Stuart. One was directed, from the beginning of the war, by Captain Thomas Nelson Conrad, chaplain of the 3rd Virginia Cavalry, the other by Frank Stringfellow, 4th Virginia Cavalry, organized somewhat later in the war. Both Conrad and Stringfellow were skilled and daring secret agents, personally gathering a great deal of the information they supplied.

Though Captain Conrad did a chaplain's ordinary duty as spiritual advisor, he frequently rode into combat with the troops or went out on missions as a uniformed scout. But his most important service to the Confederacy was spying in Washington or lurking in a Confederate secret service hideout along the banks of the Potomac, from which he sent his secret reports on to Richmond. Besides directing his own subordinate secret agents—one of whom was ostensibly working for General Lafayette C. Baker in the Federal counterintelligence service—he managed a courier line that was never broken; and he did a great deal of important espionage himself.

Though Conrad and Mrs. Greenhow may, for a time, have used the same line of communication, their networks were entirely separate. Both later published accounts of their exploits without any reference to other networks. Neither seems to have been aware of what the other was doing. The wisdom of this complete separation was demonstrated after Mrs. Greenhow had been arrested and her network broken up. Conrad and his agents, undiscovered by the Federals, could spy right on and their couriers could continue their dangerous errands undisturbed until the war was over.

Born in Virginia, Thomas Conrad went north to study, as many Southern students did, and graduated from Dickinson College in Carlisle, Pennsylvania. In those days, Dickinson, though it is in Pennsylvania, had more Southern than Northern students. Conrad's roommate was another Virginian, Mountjoy Cloud, who later became a much-trusted associate in the spy ring. In 1860, when the prewar excitement was at its height, Conrad took an M.A. and then became head of a school in Georgetown, just across Rock Creek from Washington, now part of the capital city.

The boys in his school, like most people in Georgetown, were staunch Confederates who made no effort to conceal their sympathies. Indeed, a Federal spy reported that Conrad's pupils were passing secret messages across the Potomac from the school's windows—though it is doubtful that young boys still in school had any very important military information to communicate. Possibly the principal himself was already spying. He was suspected of sending recruits to the Confederate Army.

Though the school's Southern sympathies had thus been known for a long time, not until Commencement Day in June of 1861 did the patience of the Federal authorities at last wear thin. Conrad was well known as "too pronounced" in his secessionist views. And now, some of his boys' Commencement orations smacked of the strongest Southern sentiment. Worse still, at the close of the program, the band struck up "Dixie," and emotions overflowed. Cheer after cheer sounded through the hall. Southerners stood up on their chairs, frantically waving their handkerchiefs.

That evening a squad of Yankee soldiers called upon Conrad, handcuffed him, and marched him off to the Old Capitol Prison. He was charged with communication with the enemy and sending recruits to the Confederate Army.

The Federal authorities, tolerant and easy-going at this early stage of the conflict, paroled the schoolmaster after a few days. He was allowed to wander about the capital for a month and a half, seeing all that went on, and was required only to report weekly to the authorities. Naturally, as Conrad later remarked, he "proceeded to get into more mischief without delay."

It was serious mischief. Devoutly religious though he was, Conrad joined a plot to assassinate General Winfield Scott, Commander-in-Chief of the Union Army. But when the central Confederate government in Richmond was informed of the plot, it ordered that there must be no murder.

The Reverend Major Dabney Ball, chaplain of the Confederate Cavalry Corps, took Conrad to General Stuart in July, 1861. Ball proposed Conrad as a cavalry chaplain, though he was not an ordained clergyman but a "lay reader" in the Methodist church.

Stuart agreed to Major Ball's proposal and at once assigned the new spiritual director to scouting duty. This at first meant ordinary reconnoissance, then almost continual espionage. Until the end of the war, Conrad rode through the Virginia woods and swamps he had known from boyhood, hovering along the line of the Union outguards as an ordinary scout, or secretly entering the Union lines, and often visiting Washington. But in spite of all that, he also fulfilled the ordinary duties of a chaplain whenever he could take time off from intelligence and espionage.

Immediately after Bull Run, he began to amuse himself by exchanging the Confederate uniform he wore while reconnoitering for a sober "straight-breasted coat of black cloth" in which he could pose as a Federal chaplain. In this garb, he had no difficulty in being accepted as such by Federal soldiers; and since a chaplain's duties take him everywhere, he could linger in their camps, enter the headquarters of their commanders, talk with everyone without arousing suspicion. He was so successful as a secret agent that General Stuart sent him again and again to the higher Union headquarters "to pick up any possible information" about the Union Army's intentions and movements.

According to Conrad, General Stuart employed numerous other secret agents, few of whom were ever detected by Union intelligence officers. Part of the success of these spies may have been due to Stuart's habit of denouncing them himself as Confederate deserters. Conrad was convinced that Stuart's denunciations of his own loyal secret agents as deserters from the Confederate Army saved many of them from suspicion, capture, court-martial, and an ignominious death.

Captain Conrad himself had barely departed on his first secret mission when Stuart called in Major Ball.

"Well, Major," he said, "your man Conrad was a fine specimen. He has deserted and there is no telling what information he has carried to Washington."

"Impossible!" said Ball, and eventually Stuart had to admit that he didn't really mean it.

Before long the spying chaplain was ordered to Richmond for special duty. The Southern Secretary of War, Judah P. Benjamin, sent him to Washington to meet two commissioners, one French, the other British, who had come secretly to negotiate a three-million-dollar loan for the Confederacy. The South needed money to carry on its war, and England and France were hoping the South would win, mainly because of the cotton and tobacco that came from the Southern states. Because of the Federal blockade of Southern ports, the two foreign officials went first to Washington, posing as ordinary travelers. Conrad was ordered to approach them there, get them safely across the lines, and start them on their way to Richmond. This was his first venture back into Washington as a secret agent.

Before he left, the War Department in Richmond had provided Conrad with a pass, which he himself dictated:

> War Department, Richmond, Va.
> The bearer, who may be known by a gash in his tongue and a scar upon the index finger of his left hand, has the confidence of this department.

That would take him through the Confederate lines and would identify him to the foreign emissaries as an authorized agent of the Confederacy. (It would also identify him to the Federals and would earn him the end of a rope, if captured.)

Undisturbed by this possibility—and undisturbed, too, by the Federal counterintelligence agencies—Conrad proceeded at his leisure to Washington. His beard, originally full, was now trimmed. His chin was shaven but surrounded by side whiskers. (Later on, when he felt that he might become known by this striking style of facial adornment, he changed to a heavy mustache and a long imperial.) He was careful to buy Northern shoes, which differed from those worn in the South, a difference for which Northern detectives were always watching. He also exchanged the plug tobacco of the South for the "short cut" used by Northerners.

The Confederate signal service kept a boat ready at its secret station on the Potomac some miles below Washington, so that traveling spies were always sure of a safe and easy crossing. Conrad took the precaution of waiting for low tide before landing on the Maryland shore and then walked through the mud, so that the next tide would obliterate his footprints.

He passed his parents' house in Maryland without stopping, knowing that Union sympathizers were likely to watch the homes of Confederate sympathizers. Instead, he stopped at the tavern of John Harrison Surratt, whose wife was hanged a few years later for her alleged participation in the Lincoln assassination plot. Until Surratt's death, the tavern was a rendezvous for passing Confederate spies.

Hiring a horse there and dressing himself to look like a Maryland farmer, Conrad drove unchallenged into Washington, where he put up at a hotel on Pennsylvania Avenue much frequented by visiting countryfolk. By inspecting the register of one hotel after another, he soon found the foreign negotiators at Willard's Hotel, showed them his secret pass, exhibited his scarred finger, and stuck out his tongue.

Taking their shoes and their most important papers, Conrad went to a trustworthy cobbler, who hollowed out the heels, inserted the papers, and nailed the heels back on again. Then, after buying a carriage and pair, he drove the two foreigners past the White House, past McClellan's headquarters, and on out of the city.

Along the Potomac River, a farmer with Confederate sympathies, who had already agreed to put the party across the river whenever Conrad wished, summoned a trusted slave. After giving the travelers a good midnight snack, he saw them off. Conrad gave the slave a ten-dollar gold piece, and the party of three followed him to an unguarded ford where the Negro splashed ahead on his horse to show where the water was shallow enough to ford.

They rode on and about dawn met a Confederate

guard, who passed them through to the rear. With an armed escort, the two foreign financiers rode on to Leesburg, where they took a train to Richmond.

After getting his French and British charges across the Potomac and starting them on their way to Richmond, Conrad took a stage at Poolesville, Maryland, and returned to Washington to get more information that he knew General Stuart wanted.

It did not take him long. "Trusted Southern sympathizers" were still working in the Federal War Department, under Secretary Stanton's very nose. Conrad was able to send word to Stuart that General McClellan was planning to move up the "Peninsula" against Richmond, the Confederate capital—as he soon did.

However, it was not enough that Stuart should know where McClellan and his army meant to advance; the Southern leaders also had to know what his exact strength would be. Conrad was continually hurrying back and forth on these errands.

One of Conrad's spies inside the War Department in Washington had direct access to the strength reports Stuart wanted. But the spy had to be careful. He dared not be seen leafing through such secret papers, which came from McClellan's own headquarters. Eventually, after an anxious three-day wait, Conrad received word that a summary of the reports would be lying on the desk of one of his subagents in the War Department at a certain hour next day.

The two spies did not even need to meet. The War Department man left the summary on his desk, as agreed, and went out to lunch. Captain Conrad, who knew exactly where to go, walked boldly through the

Department's crowded corridors and winked at his friend who passed on his way to lunch. Conrad went to the man's desk, found the top secret paper, and had it in Richmond two days later.

Conrad said afterward that, throughout the Peninsular Campaign, the Southern command knew just what forces McClellan had, down to the exact number of pieces of artillery.

It was an embarrassingly long time—probably a few weeks—before the Union command found out how much information the Confederates had. At the front in Virginia, Union troops finally captured Lieutenant J. Barroll Washington, aide-de-camp to General Joseph E. Johnston, who had in his possession a complete and alarmingly accurate Order of Battle of the Army of the Potomac. This gave correct corps, division, and brigade organization, and listed the correct regiments for each brigade. It also gave the names of division and brigade commanders and the approximate strength of each regiment. The captured lieutenant also had a map of the country around the Chickahominy, giving all Union positions. These were so completely up-to-date that divisional positions that had been changed only two days before were correctly shown.

Such details as this young officer carried could have come only from Southern spies with access to the files at higher Union headquarters. They were almost certainly based on the information that Conrad had smuggled out of the War Department in Washington.

At a fairly early stage in his espionage, Conrad had begun to use the old Van Ness house in Washington as his secret headquarters. This was a mansion built by

General John Peter Van Ness, a prominent politician, in the early 1800s, where the Pan-American Building now stands. At the time of the Civil War it was owned by an enthusiastic Confederate sympathizer named Thomas Green. Being isolated in spacious grounds, secure, in sympathetic hands, and only a few blocks from the White House and War Department, it was an ideal base for Conrad's intelligence ring within the enemy's capital.

But Conrad also established a more hidden retreat. He built a small shanty he called "Eagle's Nest" on a high cliff near Boyd's Hole on the south bank of the Potomac, placing mines in adjoining creeks and coves to prevent Yankee gunboats from interfering. Five men were stationed here. Conrad arranged for the already existing "Doctor's Line" to pick up messages in Washington and take them to a point on the Maryland side of the Potomac opposite the shanty. In this way he could send a secret dispatch from Washington to the Confederate capital in Richmond in less than twenty-four hours. He himself could ride straight from the front door of the Federal War Department in Washington to the front door of the Confederate War Department in Richmond in twenty-four hours. Through him or by him, messages passed back and forth without interruption until the end of the war, and not one of his messages was ever intercepted.

Such complete success could not be expected to last forever, but it did last a surprisingly long time. The Civil War was nearly half over before detectives working for Lafayette C. Baker, chief of Union counterintelligence, picked up Conrad's trail and eventually even learned his name. Although this made his work a little more difficult, it didn't really matter very much to Conrad. For one of his own Confederate spies, who had managed to worm his way into Baker's Federal counterespionage organization, was able to warn the Confederate captain in time. This daring man was named Edward Norton. No one knows anything about him except that he was a Confederate who had settled in Washington and joined the Union secret service, so that he could work as a Confederate spy from inside the Federal government. No one ever discovered what he was really doing.

Realizing that with Baker on his trail he would not be able to accomplish anything in Washington, Conrad decided to disappear until the hunt died down. With characteristic audacity, however, he saw in his own danger a fine chance to make Baker think that the Confederate spy Norton was a true-blue Union man. He instructed Norton to make a full report to Baker, in which he was to show that Conrad really was a rebel spy. This would clear Norton of any suspicion and would give an appearance of loyalty to his work. It also gave Norton a fine excuse for meeting Conrad occasionally, ostensibly to spy on him, and this made it easier for Norton to pass on to the Confederates whatever information he had picked up while working as a Federal detective!

Late one evening, Norton met Conrad at a rendezvous outside the Patent Office with a last-minute warning. Baker was about to raid the Van Ness house. Conrad would have to leave Washington at once, and at the moment he had very little money with him.

Luckily, he was able to borrow $150 from a Confederate woman in Washington. With this he paid the captain of a river schooner for his passage, pretended to be the ship's cook when a Federal boarding officer checked the boat at Alexandria, and was able to report personally to General Jeb Stuart that same morning.

Norton had warned him just in time. Baker's men began ransacking the Van Ness house within an hour after Captain Conrad left.

Like all spies in wartime, Conrad lived from one tight moment to the next. Some time after this escape, he was caught in disguise by a Federal patrol and held to await investigation. As yet, the Union men did not know he was a spy and held him merely on general suspicion. But Conrad knew his disguise would never stand investigation. To frighten off investigators, he feigned symptoms of smallpox. But this only got him from one danger into another. His captors placed him in isolation—among some genuine smallpox patients! He had to get out of there or he really would have smallpox!

Again, with a bit of luck, Conrad was able to slip away unobserved, because the guards themselves had no desire to stay close to the smallpox camp. He then began his long walk back to his retreat. Moving only at night, sleeping by day in thick woods, he finally arrived at his "safe house," Eagle's Nest.

He stayed there for a time and kept out of Washington, leaving Norton to attend to espionage in the capital. He received Norton's reports and sent them on to Confederate headquarters.

But in June of 1863, he again ventured into Washington to get information that might help General Robert E. Lee in his march to Gettysburg. Finding the city almost stripped of its defenses, he rode out to meet Stuart's raiders, whose swift ride northward would soon bring them almost in sight of the capital. If he had not missed Stuart in Maryland by an hour or two, the Confederates would probably have won at Gettysburg and thus might perhaps have won the war. It was Conrad's second misadventure of the sort, one of the many "ifs" in history.

In the spring of 1864, he again entered Washington in civilian clothes, visited Union General Burnside's IX Corps at Annapolis, wearing a Federal chaplain's uniform, then returned to the capital once more to verify his information. This secret reconnoissance provided an important part of the intelligence that enabled General Lee to anticipate, with such astonishing accuracy, Grant's advance into the Wilderness before the frightful battle there began.

8

Stuart's Spy, Stringfellow, and His Friends

Captain Conrad's espionage was ably supplemented by a second group of scouts and spies in General Stuart's intelligence service. After the war, Frank Stringfellow became the best known of the group. Stringfellow was a suitable colleague for the Reverend Captain Conrad. Though not yet ordained, he became a clergyman of the Episcopal church after the war. He possessed all Conrad's religious zeal, plus all his boldness and skill in espionage.

Conrad's and Stringfellow's almost incredible adventures were really commonplaces in the lives of Stuart's spies. Such records as survive suggest that they were all equally bold and equally adventurous. But Conrad, who wrote two books, and Stringfellow, who gave lectures on his wartime adventures to earn money for his church, are the only ones who became widely known. Captain (later Colonel) John Burke talked sometimes of his adventures, and a few who listened thought to make notes—but far too few.

Stringfellow's full name was Benjamin Franklin

Stringfellow. When the war broke out, he was teaching Latin and Greek at a girls' school in Mississippi. With his gray-blue eyes, blond hair that curled a little, and very slight stature—he weighed only ninety-four pounds—he was not an impressive military figure. But that turned out to be an advantage. Made up properly, he could (and did) enter the Union lines disguised as a girl and return with his masquerade unquestioned. His slight stature also led numerous incautious Federals to suppose he was harmless—until it was too late.

In September of 1861, General Jeb Stuart was operating a cavalry screen around Dranesville, northwest of Washington, to check the comings and goings of Union spies and give the Confederates early warning of any Union troop movements. Working with these uniformed troops, a group of disguised Confederate spies moved farther on ahead, into the Federal lines. Besides Stringfellow, this group included John Burke and Redmond Burke. Redmond Burke was said to have trained Stringfellow in scouting (but not in espionage), and on one occasion to have saved his life. There was also Will Farley, a low-voiced, mild-mannered South Carolinian of medium height and handsome features, who was kept on Stuart's own staff "for such service as was needed," because he was regarded as one of the most desperate fighters in the whole command. The famous John Mosby was another, and there were many more, equally daring but less known.

Mosby had begun the war as a cavalry lieutenant. His energy and activity soon earned him a reputation, but he was not "an easy or indulgent officer," and he was not re-elected as an officer in his company. Lieutenant

Mosby would have suffered the humiliation of being "busted back" to private if General Stuart had not assigned him as a reconnoissance officer. After that he rose swiftly to success as a cavalry raider and guerrilla, employing some skillful spies himself and, incidentally, winning the hearty admiration of his leading foeman, General Ulysses S. Grant.

Sometime in 1861, Stringfellow was sent to the Stone House Hotel at Manassas to meet E. Pliny Bryan, a telegrapher in the Confederate Signal Service. This service not only controlled ordinary army signals but also co-operated with the spies and handled secret communications under the central government in Richmond.

Bryan was being sent as a spy to deal mainly with the Northern press. In the beginning, the Confederates had tried to discover the Union Army's strength by having secret agents keep an eye on troops arriving in Washington, but they could not be sure how many troops were being passed around the city instead of through it. They soon discovered they could learn a great deal more by reading the Northern newspapers, which gave news of Union troop movements—as if loyal Northerners were the only people who could read them! Confederate sympathizers all over the North collected newspapers. Bryan and other secret agents like him searched these for military information, which they sent on to Richmond. From the Northern press, a Confederate signal officer said, "We learned not only of all arrivals, but also of assignments to brigades and divisions, and, by tabulating these, we always knew quite accurately the strength of the enemy's army." Since the Constitution of the United States guarantees the freedom of the press, it is hard to keep dangerous news out of the papers in time of war.

One of Bryan's agents was a dentist in Alexandria. Stringfellow later gave his name as Richard M. Sykes, but this was a pseudonym. Stringfellow habitually concealed the names of civilians who had helped him, even after the war was over.

Stringfellow lived with this man—whatever his name—posing as his dental apprentice and assistant for some time. He knew nothing about dentistry, but that couldn't be helped. In those days, few young men went to dental, medical, or law schools. Instead, they entered the offices of dentists, doctors, and lawyers as apprentices, and learned their professions there.

To give Stringfellow the utmost possible security, an elaborate "cover story" had been worked out for him. He was to assume the name of Edward Delcher, a real man of about Stringfellow's age, who had been, until shortly before, a dentist's apprentice in Baltimore. But as Delcher was now a soldier on duty along the Mississippi River, he would hardly turn up at an embarrassing moment.

Bryan had thought of everything and had planned Stringfellow's work with meticulous care. Any inquisitive Federal security man snooping about Baltimore would discover that there really had been a dental assistant named Edward Delcher. Being personally acquainted with the real Delcher family, Bryan was able to provide Stringfellow with a baptismal certificate made out in Edward Delcher's name. He also provided a medical certificate showing that the supposed Edward Delcher was unfit for military service. This was meant to answer any possible question why so young a man as Stringfellow was not in the army. If he ever had to produce it, his deceptively frail physique would confirm it.

To make sure his disguise was perfect, Stringfellow wore a civilian suit that had once belonged to the man he was impersonating and bore the label of a Baltimore tailor. He was also given a vast amount of detail regarding the Delcher family, the kind of intimate information no one but a relative was likely to have. Stringfellow memorized all this so that he would be able to answer, offhand, any test questions.

A local resident living on the outskirts of Alexandria, a few miles south of Washington, whose name Stringfellow gave as Sam Whiteside—no doubt another cover name—guided the young man through the Federal outposts to his own home. As they approached the house, Whiteside went ahead alone, leaving Stringfellow a little way behind him. After he had made sure no untrustworthy neighbors or Union soldiers had come in his absence, Whiteside summoned Stringfellow.

The Confederate spy spent the rest of the day hidden in the Whiteside house, studying the little black notebook Bryan had given him containing all the minute details the new Edward Delcher had to know. Then he was ready to start out in his new life of being somebody else and having to remember it every moment. Nothing must slip. Bryan had prepared him carefully.

In Dr. Sykes's home in Alexandria, Stringfellow found an old well under the floor. By lifting a board, he could drop in great quantities of newspapers. Here they could pile up without drawing the prying eye of some caller or patient who might wonder why so many newspapers had been allowed to accumulate. Each night Stringfellow placed in an envelope his summary of the military information he had gleaned from the papers. He left this in a letterdrop under the eaves of the doctor's office. Each morning it was gone. Probably the courier who collected the messages was part of Mrs. Greenhow's network, as she reported to Richmond about that time that "a line of daily communication is now open through Alexandria."

Stringfellow stayed with the dentist through the early part of 1862 without any real danger, though there were some nerve-wracking episodes. Once, in February, an emergency patient with a towel wrapped around his jaw entered while a Federal major was in the waiting room. The new arrival appeared to be in great pain. It was easy to suppose that his jaw was badly swollen, as he had a towel wrapped round it. That concealed his face, and it didn't occur to anybody that there might be good reasons why he didn't want people to see his face. Since the major seemed to be in intense pain, he received immediate treatment, and during his treatment agonizing sounds came from the dentist's office. Then the man departed through the waiting room, still with that towel.

This man's suffering and his treatment were pure pretense. He was a Confederate secret agent, bringing a special report of such urgency that he had to take the risk of visiting the dentist's office by daylight. It was alarming to find an officer in a blue uniform sitting there, but all his realistic acting fooled the Federal major completely. The information this spy brought gave the Confederate Army warning of a proposed attack in time to move troops to a safer position.

Personal complications now arose, which might easily have revealed Stringfellow for what he was. He had been careful not to go near Emma Green, the Alexandria girl he meant to marry—had not, in fact, even allowed her to know he was in town. By chance, however, Emma took her grandfather to Dr. Sykes, and Stringfellow happened to be in the outer office when she came in. Naturally, she greeted him with delighted amazement. To make matters worse, one of the patients in the waiting room was a Pinkerton operative.

There was only one thing for Stringfellow to do. Hoping that Emma would understand the situation, he coldly told the girl he loved that he did not know her at all. There must be some mistake. He had never seen her before.

Emma was as quick-witted as he. She apologized prettily. A chance resemblance had misled her. Yes, indeed, she had mistaken Mr. Delcher for someone else. She was very sorry. Emma had no idea what all this meant, but she trusted her Frank. When her grandfather's treatment was over, she took him home and asked no questions.

There were other complexities. Both Bryan and Stringfellow had always feared the dentist's wife, the daughter of a Union officer. They were afraid that, if she came to suspect Stringfellow, she might report him to the provost marshal. She did, in fact, soon guess the truth, but she did not report him as a spy; she did something else equally dangerous.

Stringfellow had for some time noticed that the lady seemed much too friendly. The doctor had noticed it, too, and his manner toward his apprentice became cold. Though the dentist's wife had, in fact, no special interest in Stringfellow, she was beginning to feel that her husband was growing indifferent toward her. She wanted to make him jealous. She succeeded only too well.

Suddenly one night she went to Stringfellow's room with alarming news. Her husband was at that very moment on his way to betray Stringfellow to the Union authorities. The spy quickly prepared to flee, but upon reaching the door, heard cavalry moving in the street. Were they coming for him? Stringfellow did not wait to find out. He rushed to the rear, away from the street along which the troopers were riding, climbed through a window, and headed for the Whiteside home as fast as he could go.

When he came within sight of it, he watched from an adjoining hill. It was well he did. Before long, Union cavalry appeared, searched the Whiteside house and barn, then rode away baffled. Only when he was sure the last Yank was gone did the spy enter. Then he learned that Whiteside had been killed since Stringfellow had been there last, but his widow had kept Stringfellow's uniform ready for him. Once again in gray, he was no longer a spy and could not be legally hanged, but he could still be made a prisoner of war. Striking out for the Confederate lines at Fredericksburg, he reached them safely, though only after a chase by Union cavalry.

Rejoining General Stuart was difficult. There was no rail transportation; General Johnston's retreating army was using all the trains there were. Eventually, Stringfellow found Jeb and his horsemen near Yorktown, Virginia. It was about mid-April, 1862.

For some time, Stringfellow was busy with ordinary cavalry scouting in proper uniform. With John Mosby and one of the Burkes, he reconnoitered around McClellan's army in mid-June, after which Stuart mentioned him in dispatches as "particularly conspicuous for gallantry and efficiency."

As Stuart's scouts and spies, these men played a large part in the series of Confederate victories that followed during that summer. Important information for the Confederate generals was pouring in from Stringfellow and Burke, who were now practically living with the enemy, in constant danger.

Traveling at night and hiding in the daytime, they penetrated far behind the Union lines without being discovered. Once Stringfellow, who disliked this part of his job, had to knock a sleeping Federal picket unconscious. When he recovered his senses, the victim turned out to be a loquacious fellow, perfectly willing to tell all he knew, and revealed a great deal of useful military information. The man was not moved by lofty patriotic fervor; he told Stringfellow he had joined the army mainly to get away from his wife. From his talk Stringfellow gained important advance information about the Federals' next move, with the result that Stonewall Jackson soon knew the enemy general's intentions and capabilities. In this case, it was General Pope's plans and strength that concerned him.

At this time, during the fighting at Cedar Mountain, Stringfellow was near his own home, but he took no heedless risks, even to see his mother. He stayed in a thicket behind the Union lines, and though—as the Grays drove the Yankees back—the boys in blue came unpleasantly close to the spy's hiding place, they did not catch him.

That night, he was startled to see fresh Union troops

approaching. In the moonlight, he could not be quite sure of their numbers, but the long column looked like an army corps. If a whole new corps was really coming in, he had important intelligence, but he needed to verify it. Prowling about in the dark, he caught a prisoner. Yes, the man told him, these were new Federal troops; Sigel's I Corps was arriving from Sperryville to reinforce Pope.

A whole new corps! Stonewall must have this news at once.

Regretfully knocking the man on the head—the only possible alternative to killing him outright—Stringfellow watched the approaching Federal corps a little longer, then hurried back to Confederate headquarters with the news. On his dangerous way through the blue-clad army he was challenged only once.

"What regiment?"

"Pennsylvania Bucktails," replied the Confederate spy, having just learned from the soldier he had knocked out that this famous regiment was in the area. The Union sentry let him pass.

From time to time, Stringfellow made trips to Washington, and on these journeys he could stop in Alexandria to see Emma Green. On one of these visits he had a very close call. When he was about ready to return to Confederate headquarters to report, his career was nearly ended by pure bad luck. Rounding a corner hastily, he almost bumped into a Federal captain he had helped capture the year before. It was still light, and each recognized the other instantly.

Stringfellow fled; the officer shouted and ran after him. As he fled, Stringfellow saw the open door of a house into which he dashed. Luckily, he knew whose it was. He came upon a calm old lady of Southern leanings, a friend of his mother's, who sat mending a tablecloth.

She grasped the situation and lifted one edge of her enormous hoopskirt.

"Here, Frank," she said, and draping her tentlike skirt around the crouching spy, she went on mending.

Breathless men in blue uniforms arrived at once with questions. Yes, the lady said, someone had dashed through the house and apparently out the back door. The baffled pursuers searched in vain and withdrew with apologies.

After the war and after Stringfellow had married his Emma and had become an Episcopal rector, he told in his lectures of these adventures and many others. In describing the dangers of the secret service he once told a friend that he had never gone on any of his dangerous secret missions expecting to come back alive. But he did come back, and lived a long and useful life as a civilian, when all his desperate adventures were over.

9

The Master Wiretapper

The star wiretapper of the whole Civil War was George A. Ellsworth, a telegrapher born in Canada, who accompanied General John Hunt Morgan on his raids into Kentucky. Ellsworth met Morgan in Mobile, Alabama, and joined his cavalry there. General Beauregard, who often managed to fill Union generals with spectacularly false information and who appreciated a talent for fooling others, recognized Ellsworth's peculiar abilities. Morgan, Beauregard, and Ellsworth seem to have had a great deal of fun deceiving, and planning how to deceive, the Northerners, while winning many victories for the South. Ellsworth's part in this was intercepting the Federals' telegraph messages, cutting telegraph wires, sending false messages, and thus causing alarm, confusion, or delay.

In the spring of 1862, General Beauregard thought up a new scheme, which completely deceived the Union command at Corinth, Tennessee. Knowing that General Halleck was preparing to attack him with Union forces much greater than his own, Beauregard scared the Union general off by an ingenious trick. He ordered a great many trains to pull into Corinth with as much whistling and noise as possible. Each train was greeted with resounding Confederate cheers. The Federals, lying outside Corinth, could hear this perpetual uproar and attributed it to incoming reinforcements for Beauregard —just what Beauregard wanted them to think.

All the noise really indicated the gradual withdrawal of Beauregard's army. Departing trains, heavily loaded with troops in gray, slipped out of Corinth in silence. These same trains, returning empty to carry away more troops, received all the cheers. Beauregard was steadily getting his troops away from Corinth, in complete secrecy.

But his bluff did not deceive the railroad men serving the Union Army. They convinced Major General U. S. Grant that the Confederates were secretly evacuating. An expert, they told him, could tell by putting an ear down to the rails, "not only which way the trains were moving, but which trains were loaded and which were empty." Loaded trains had been going out for several days, they said, and empty ones were coming back in, regardless of the cheers. The sounds of the wheels on the track were different. But Grant could not convince General Halleck, and at this time Halleck was his commander.

General Halleck was completely fooled by Beauregard's tricks. He believed everything his enemy wanted him to believe. The clever Beauregard thus got all his troops away without a battle and escaped almost certain defeat.

Just after this, on June 1, 1862, George Ellsworth, former assistant superintendent of the Texas Telegraph

Company, enlisted in Company A, 2nd Kentucky Cavalry, then in Chattanooga. On July 1, he was put on special duty as telegraph operator and promoted to captain. Within a short time, Ellsworth was with the raiding column that the guerrilla fighter General John Hunt Morgan led north into Kentucky. Morgan and Beauregard had conferred in Corinth, Morgan met Ellsworth in Mobile, and now the three gay deceivers worked more or less together.

Morgan led his men a thousand miles in less than a month. He captured and paroled twelve hundred prisoners, while losing only one hundred of his eight hundred troopers. A large part of this success was due to the clever lies Ellsworth sent to various Union telegraph stations. Befuddled by these adroit falsehoods, the Federals rarely knew where Morgan was and never knew what he was going to do next. The relish with which Ellsworth describes the pranks he played during this and other raids and some of the jocular messages General Morgan telegraphed across the lines to enemy commanders show that the two shared the same delight in tricking the Federals.

Messages sent by Ellsworth confused and delayed the Yankees, while the Yankee messages he picked up by tapping the wires warned Morgan well in advance what the enemy was doing or was going to do. General Morgan succeeded largely because of the information Ellsworth thus secured; but he also found it diverting to delude the Union leaders.

When the column reached Cave City, Kentucky, about dusk, Morgan himself led a detail of ten or fifteen men, including Ellsworth, toward the Louisville & Nashville Railroad, a vital Union supply line. Being largely limestone country, Kentucky is full of caves, and one well-known cavern, Horse Cave, was near the railroad. About half a mile away from this landmark, with a heavy thunderstorm approaching, Morgan halted his little band, while Ellsworth cut into the Louisville–Bowling Green telegraph line so carefully that the Louisville operator, who was sending at that very moment, noticed nothing.

The first word Ellsworth heard being tapped was "Morgan." After listening a moment or two, he realized that the Union commander, General Jeremiah T. Boyle, at Louisville, was telegraphing orders to Union Colonel Sanders D. Bruce at Bowling Green, to pursue and capture the Morgan raiders.

But these orders never reached Colonel Bruce, nor did any other messages sent to Federal operators south of Horse Cave reach their destination that night, for Ellsworth intercepted all telegrams. But it would never do for the Federals to know that all their messages were ending in enemy hands. Hence, with Morgan's personal assistance, Ellsworth concocted replies to make the Federals think their messages were being received as usual.

During this adventure, Ellsworth acquired the nickname "Lightning" which clung to him for the rest of the war. The story goes that a thunderstorm broke not long after he had tapped the wire, and he sat at his instrument in the darkness with electricity playing around him. A suspicious Federal operator, listening to Ellsworth's messages, found his touch on the telegraph keys unfamiliar, and queried, "Who are you? And what's the matter with your office?" Ellsworth replied, "O.K., lightning," meaning that lightning was interfering with the telegraphic current. After that, he was known to the Confederates as "Captain Lightning" or "Morgan's Lightning."

Sitting through two hours or more on a rainy night, with water up to his knees, Ellsworth listened to messages from Louisville, Nashville, and other towns—though none of these messages went beyond the point where he had cut the wire. Many of them were commercial telegrams, countermanding shipments of money and valuables lest Morgan's raiders lay hands on them. Later, when Union operators and businessmen found out what had happened, all these messages had to be sent over again. This overburdened the wires, caused general confusion, and added to the Federals' troubles—exactly what the Confederates wanted.

Of much greater importance was a message which Morgan intended to be false but which, by pure accident, turned out to be true. He had Ellsworth tick out a dispatch, supposedly from Union headquarters in Nashville, to Union headquarters in Louisville. This reported that Morgan was somewhere near Gallatin, Tennessee, when he was actually near Cave City, Kentucky, fifty or sixty miles away. Then he added that General Nathan Bedford Forrest's Confederate cavalry had attacked Murfreesboro and was now advancing on Nashville.

Morgan had no idea what Forrest was doing. He was making it all up, and his report of the raid on Murfreesboro was his own invention. All he meant to do was worry the Yankees. When, by pure coincidence, Forrest really did attack Murfreesboro a few days later on July 13, that made all the other fabrications seem authentic!

Within three or four miles of Lebanon, about dusk on July 11, Morgan's raiding column was fired on by Union Home Guards, who put up such a strong resistance that Morgan could not enter the town itself until two or three in the morning. Then, with Morgan, Ellsworth went to the telegraph office. A light was burning and the office appeared to have been deserted a short time before. The telegraph key was silent, although everything was ready to receive or send a message.

But within a few minutes the clicking began, and some office signing itself "Z" started calling office "B." Ellsworth did not know where either office was, but he gave the usual answer indicating that an operator was ready to receive: "I.I."

Immediately Z asked, "What of the marauders now?"

The Lebanon telegraph office, which Ellsworth now occupied, was the natural place to send such a message. Ellsworth assumed, correctly, that B meant Lebanon. He replied briefly that the Union forces in Lebanon (which, in fact, had long since fled) were "holding them at bay." Z then volunteered the information that eight hundred Union soldiers were on their way to Lebanon to help defend it against Morgan's raiders.

It was important news to Morgan to know that he might have to fight eight hundred additional Yankees. The eight hundred were at Z. But where was Z? Ellsworth had to find out quickly what town was represented by that call letter. The Federal telegraph operator at Lebanon, D. E. Martyn, could have supplied the information. But he had escaped just ahead of Morgan's men and was at that moment crouching by a small, smelly stream, while Ellsworth was occupying his office chair.

Few Union messages were going through at that early morning hour, and the key was silent. Ellsworth improved the time by reading the office file of dispatches of the day before. Among them, he found a message to General Boyle in Louisville, reporting that four hundred "marauders"—that meant Confederates, of course—were approaching Lebanon. This wasn't true. Morgan's men were nowhere near Lebanon as yet. But it was good news for the Confederates. General Boyle and his Federals would now be puzzled by having two locations for Morgan's men—Gallatin, Tennessee, and Lebanon, Kentucky, many miles apart.

Ellsworth now picked up further news that Union troops of the 60th Indiana were on their way to Lebanon. Presumably, these were the promised reinforcements. So Morgan sent out a special detachment to destroy the only bridge over which the 60th Indiana could pass.

Presently Z sent another query: "What news? Any more skirmishes after your last message?"

Ellsworth replied, "We drove what little cavalry there was away."

Z now inquired whether "the train" had arrived yet. Ellsworth said no, it hadn't; and, by the way, how many troops were aboard it? Five hundred, said Z, 60th Indiana, Colonel Owens commanding. At least, five hundred Yankees weren't as dangerous as eight hundred.

This was more useful information for Morgan, but it grew increasingly important to know where station Z was. General Morgan wanted Ellsworth to ask the question outright, but Ellsworth pointed out that any real Union operator at Lebanon would know, and such a question would give their game away.

Then Ellsworth had an idea. He tapped out that a "gentleman here in the office" had bet him some cigars that Z could not spell the name of the town where his station was located.

Z, who turned out to be W. H. Drake, night operator, rose like a fish to the bait.

"L-e-b-a-n-o-n J-u-n-c-t-i-o-n," he clicked. "How did you think I would spell it?"

"He thought you would put two b's in 'Lebanon,' " replied Ellsworth.

"Ha! ha! ha!" laughed Z at the other end. "He's a green one."

"Yes, that's so," agreed Ellsworth, and he and his general had the last laugh.

But when William R. Plum, the day operator, took over an hour or two later, Ellsworth for the first time aroused suspicion at Lebanon Junction. Martyn had escaped so swiftly from the office to his hiding place by the little stream that Ellsworth had had no chance to study his style of sending. Had they been able to capture Martyn, Ellsworth might have been able to watch him at the key. Since every telegrapher has his own individual touch, other telegraphers can usually tell who the sender is. Consequently, the first fraudulent message stirred Plum's suspicions. Ellsworth's touch didn't sound like Martyn's. Worse still, Ellsworth presently replied to a casual message with an "O.K." This seemed queer to Plum. Never under any circumstances did Martyn send an "O.K." Who *was* on the other end of that wire?

Drake, who had not yet left the Lebanon Junction office, ridiculed Plum's fears. He was sure the man on the other end was Martyn, for during the night he had been talking with him by the hour. Plum was reassured and his suspicions were not aroused again when Ellsworth tapped the message that his key would be silent for a little while. He was going to take a nap. But the truth was that Morgan had, at that moment, entered the office and told Ellsworth to close it down. They must get away. Plum, in reply, merely warned B not to oversleep. While Ellsworth was supposed to be napping, he and Morgan and the troops were on their way to Versailles, Kentucky. After dark, Ellsworth went off toward Frankfort with a squad to tap the wires.

On July 15, 1862, three miles from Midway, Morgan sent Ellsworth into town ahead of the column to capture the telegraph operator there before he could send out a warning. Taking Private Cabel Maddox with him, Ellsworth walked in on the unsuspecting local operator, one J. J. Woolums. They were wearing civilian clothes.

Ellsworth noticed at once that the telegraph poles outside the building carried two wires, only one of which entered the station. When Woolums explained that the upper wire, not connected with his instruments, was the military wire, Ellsworth sent Maddox up a ladder to cut it. When Woolums who still did not realize he was a prisoner, protested, he learned the worst. The two Confederates then forced the Union operator to send an innocent telegram to Lexington. This merely asked for the correct time, but it gave Ellsworth a chance to get some idea of Woolums's style of using the key.

By the time Morgan and his troopers rode into

Midway, Ellsworth was in control of the wire, and the Federals had no chance to send any telegraphic warning. Imitating Woolums's style as best he could, Ellsworth soon found that all military messages were passing over a through wire running directly from Lexington to Frankfort. Having discovered this, he cut Frankfort off entirely and began talking to Lexington, posing as the Frankfort operator. Soon after this, a telegram arrived from a conductor in Lexington asking whether it was safe for his train to enter Midway. Seeing a chance to bring a whole train into Morgan's grasp, Ellsworth replied, "All right; come on. No signs of rebels here."

This kind of thing could not go on forever without being detected. By July 13, General Jeremiah T. Boyle, the Union commander in Louisville, who had been growing suspicious, wired the War Department: "The rebels undoubtedly have control of telegraph all around us." Even so, Ellsworth was able to continue his deception for a week longer. By sending messages announcing the strength of Morgan's troops as over a thousand more than they really were, he fooled the Federals into leaving the raiders undisturbed while they moved through Kentucky, destroying a million dollars' worth of U.S. government stores.

After abandoning the Midway office, Morgan went on to Georgetown, Kentucky, arriving there about ten o'clock that night. The local Union telegraph operator assured Ellsworth that the line had been out of order for some time. Suspecting that the Union man was lying, Ellsworth tested by a method traditional among old-time telegraphers: he touched his tongue to the wire. Currents were weak in those days, and the faint electric impulses were easier to detect on a moist, sensitive surface than with the fingers. As Ellsworth had expected, the current was still on, but the Union operators were silent, well aware now that the enemy was probably listening. More than one Union operator had become suspicious of Ellsworth's "fist," that is, his touch on the key.

When Cincinnati asked for information, Ellsworth was detected. Already suspicious, Cincinnati asked, upon being told by Ellsworth that Morgan's men were encamped right there, "How can you be in the office and not be arrested?"

"Oh," tapped Ellsworth, "I am in the dark and am reading by magnet." That was a plausible story, but not quite plausible enough to satisfy the Cincinnati man. He set a trap.

"Where is your assistant?" he asked.

"I don't know."

"Have you seen him today?"

"No," replied Ellsworth, who did not know that the real Georgetown operator had no assistant. His reply proved that there was a rebel on the Georgetown end of the line, and the Cincinnati operator probably spread the word at once.

Though Ellsworth's luck was slowly running out, it didn't matter very much by this time. Morgan was ready to turn back south with his raiders, and the Union leaders were in a state of confusion that would last till he was safe in Tennessee. Cutting in on the Federal wire at one point, Ellsworth heard the operator at Lebanon warning Lebanon Junction: "George Ellsworth, the rebel operator, may be on the line between here and Cumberland Gap."

About nine o'clock on the night of July 21, as the Confederates approached the town of Somerset, word came down the column, "Lightning to the front!" There was no response till Ellsworth was discovered, fast asleep on his horse. Morgan, as was his custom, sent the telegrapher ahead. Ellsworth was given two men to capture the Somerset telegraph office before the operator there could send out warning. An hour later, seeing only one light in the quiet country town, Ellsworth judged it must be the telegraph office, approached quietly on foot, and entered just as the Somerset operator dropped out of a back window and fled.

Ellsworth had barely taken over the key when a message came through from the Union operator, James Meager, at Stanford, Kentucky. Meager had been out repairing the line near Crab Orchard which Morgan's men had just finished cutting. He was now, unknowingly, reporting to the man responsible for breaking the line!

By this time, well aware of Ellsworth's tricks, poor Meager suggested that he and the Somerset operator ought to have a private recognition sign, so as to be sure they were talking to each other and not to Ellsworth. Ellsworth, of course, agreed to the Union operator's suggestion, and tapped back: "Before signing off we will make the figure 7."

Meager had no idea how badly he had been fooled till some of Morgan's horsemen clattered into Stanford. Then he had to run for it. He was wounded while climbing a tree, but escaped. As a friend remarked afterward, Meager had already been a prisoner of the Confederates once, and after that "there was no catching Jimmy."

Soon afterward, the puzzled Federals in Louisville were asking Ellsworth where General Morgan was. They knew he had left Crab Orchard for Somerset at 1:00 P.M. on July 21. Ellsworth replied that he had no information on Morgan, which was almost true, since he and his group had ridden far ahead of the main column, and Morgan himself had not yet reached Somerset. With this news, he succeeded in keeping the Federals quiet until the Confederates were ready to leave Somerset.

Then, since the raiding column had now nearly completed its circle and was again approaching the Tennessee border and safety, Morgan indulged his sense of humor. He gave Ellsworth a message to send to a Louisville editor, ending with the news that Morgan's raid had destroyed one million dollars' worth of government stores and was "now off for Dixie."

At the words "government stores," the Louisville operator broke in to ask what he meant. Ellsworth told him to wait for the end of the message. When it came, the signature of John H. Morgan explained everything.

Ellsworth's successful deception ought to have made the Federal telegraph operators skeptical. But when Morgan made his swift dash from Sparta, Tennessee, to Gallatin, north of Nashville, in August, 1862, Ellsworth was again able to deceive the Federals. The raid was all over and Morgan was riding south again, with the whole Federal garrison as prisoners, in two or three days.

Gallatin was then occupied by the 28th Kentucky, a Union regiment raised in that divided state, which contributed soldiers to both sides. Preliminary secret reconnoissance was entrusted to one of Morgan's many spies. Whenever possible, Morgan sent an agent ahead into any town he intended to raid, to collect information. This man rushed frantically into the town a few days before the raid, pretending to be an agitated civilian, explaining he had barely escaped being drafted into the Confederate Army and begging for refuge until the Confederate recruiting officers left the district.

Sympathetic Federals cared for the "fugitive," who was really Morgan's spy, thus giving him a fine chance to study the area and find out that Colonel William P. Boone, the regimental commander, had his quarters in the local hotel, some distance from his troops. It was no doubt this same spy who located the telegraph office and the 28th Kentucky's camp. He was playing what the Federals called a "Morganish trick."

The raiders set out August 10, 1862, and on that same day Morgan sent a certain Captain Joseph de Shea to slip into Gallatin and quietly capture Colonel Boone. With de Shea and his group of kidnapers went Ellsworth. Leaving their horses a mile outside the town, the Confederates made their way toward it on foot, hidden by the surrounding corn fields. Arriving at dawn, they found the colonel in his hotel room, dressing. They made him prisoner, assured his agitated wife he would not be injured, and departed with him.

Ellsworth knew just where to go. With one companion, he set off for the railroad station where, on the second floor, J. N. Brooks, the local ticket seller, expressman, and telegrapher, had his bedroom.

"Surrender!" bellowed Ellsworth, thundering on the door. "I demand it in the name of General Morgan."

Brooks opened up to find himself facing the barrels of four pistols. He could not possibly resist. His situation was hopeless. Though triumphant so far, Ellsworth was uncomfortably aware that he and his companion were all alone with their prisoner, only a few hundred yards from a large Union force. But soon he heard the clattering hoofs of Morgan's troopers and knew he was safe. As it was too early to use the telegraph, Ellsworth accepted his philosophical prisoner's invitation to breakfast.

With its regimental commander already in his hands, Morgan closed in at once on the sleeping 28th Kentucky. He had worked his men into a position from which their fire could destroy the whole regiment before any of its sentries discovered him. Knowing they had no chance to resist, the Kentuckians surrendered. Since Brooks, the operator, had already been caught sleeping, no word of warning to other Union forces reached the wires.

Breakfast over, Ellsworth compelled his prisoner to send a message asking about trains. Brooks complied, but used his key as awkwardly as he dared, in a style quite unlike his own, hoping to rouse suspicion at the other end. Either this clumsy sending or the unusual hour did strike Jimmy Morris, operator at Nashville Northeast, as queer. There was nothing urgent about this inquiry. Then why was Brooks getting up at half past four in the morning to send it?

Morris could not click off a warning to other operators without alerting the intruder in the Gallatin station, but he apparently sent a messenger to the nearest headquarters with word that there was something wrong at Gallatin.

Other Nashville stations were slow in getting the warning, for at 7:10 A.M., Ellsworth heard a certain Conductor Murphy asking Nashville for orders to bring his train from Franklin, Kentucky, to Gallatin, about twenty-five miles to the south across the Tennessee line. Nashville refused, but Ellsworth pricked up his ears. Making sure Nashville could not hear him, he called Murphy at Franklin, canceling the previous order and instructing him to bring his train on to Gallatin.

When Murphy's train steamed in, he found a Confederate reception committee awaiting him; Morgan's men rejoiced over the capture of twenty-eight freight cars loaded with Federal supplies, and fifty fresh horses. No Northern operator as yet knew what had happened to Conductor Murphy and his freight. The Confederates made it impossible to send reports. Nashville naturally supposed that Murphy was still obeying orders to lay over at Franklin.

Ellsworth decided to convince Union operators that, whatever might have happened to Number Six, it had not happened at Gallatin. Pretending that he himself was anxious about the train, he began asking Nashville why Number Six had not appeared.

The Nashville operator, never dreaming how truly he spoke replied, "Guess Morgan's got her; she left on time with twenty-four cars, six loaded." Then, soon after 9:00 A.M., the Federal operator at Bowling Green also began asking what had happened to Number Six.

"Not yet arrived," replied Ellsworth, cheerfully.

Soon after this, he heard Nashville announcing that another passenger train was just pulling out. About 10:45, however, Nashville suddenly became suspicious and began asking Ellsworth a series of seemingly casual questions, the real purpose of which Ellsworth recognized at once. He suspected that someone on the passenger train—which had failed to reach Gallatin as announced —had seen some Confederates, and that the train had been run back to Nashville and the Federals there had been warned. It was also likely that Jimmy Morris, at Nashville Northeast, had at last succeeded in getting a special courier through to tell the Union men of the very odd telegraphic style that Brooks, at Gallatin, had suddenly adopted.

Ellsworth had the unhappy Brooks, still a prisoner, brought into the office, and ordered him to take the key again and give correct answers to Nashville's queries. Probably poor Brooks continued to send in a style as unlike his own as possible, but he did not dare send the wrong answers. If he did, Nashville would show increasing suspicion, and Ellsworth would take him as a prisoner to Dixie. If he co-operated, he might be released when the rebels left Gallatin.

"Who is at the key?" inquired Nashville.

"B," was the reply.

"Who is B?"

"Brooks."

"What Brooks give your full name."

The full name was supplied, but still Nashville's skepticism remained.

"Who was that young lady that went with You and I to Major Fosters the other Night?" Nashville asked, ungrammatically.

"Don't know you—never went with any young lady— Don't Know Major Foster," clicked the Gallatin key.

Nashville now reported that, as Ellsworth had suspected, the passenger train to Gallatin really had been turned back. A Negro had met it four miles from Gallatin, saying "John Morgan Has the town."

With grim humor Ellsworth telegraphed orders for the unfortunate Negro, who had patriotically reported the truth, to be arrested and jailed, adding: "Everything is quiet Here."

"I am satisfied but the Superintendent is not," Nashville answered. "He wants to know What that was He sent you by express yesterday."

Brooks answered: "A jug of Nitric Acid."

"Correct the train will start again the negro has been arrested."

There was one other question.

"Mr. Marshall, the Superintendent of the Railroads, is not yet satisfied that you are not Morgan's operator, and he wishes you to tell him who you wished to take your place while you were gone on leave of absence; how long you wished to be gone, and when did you wish to go?"

Again Brooks gave his story. He had to, with Ellsworth standing over him.

"Tell Mr. Marshall I wished Mr. Clayton to take my place while I got a week's leave to go to Cincinnati."

Marshall, at last convinced that all was well, gave orders for the next north- and southbound trains to proceed as usual, his orders of course being audible to all stations along the way, including Gallatin. The Nashville train left at 11:15.

After that, routine messages followed until 4:00 P.M., when Nashville, greatly excited, called to say both trains had "returned the second time." Confederates certainly were in Gallatin, whether the telegraph operator there knew it or not. What had become of the Nashville train that was missing?

Ellsworth was evasive until about 4:00. Then Nashville called, asking who was now at the Gallatin key. Morgan himself had come into the office and Ellsworth asked him what to say.

"Tell him anything you please," said Morgan. They would be leaving at 5:00. The Confederates had given up hope of capturing another train.

"I am Ellsworth," the telegrapher confessed to Nashville.

"You d——m wild Canadian what are you doing there," tapped Nashville Northeast in reply.

Laden with booty, Morgan's cavaliers withdrew to Hartsville, Tennessee, with a sense of a job well done. Before leaving Gallatin, Ellsworth took Brooks's pocketbook, which had forty dollars in it, as legitimate spoils of war. He also seized fifty or sixty dollars that he found in the telegraph office. Brooks protested to Morgan, who made Ellsworth return the pocketbook and its contents, plus Brooks's new coat and shirt.

Though the Federals were now on their guard against Ellsworth, he continued to work with Morgan. Some time later in the winter, in January, 1863, Ellsworth ventured once more into Kentucky, this time in disguise, tapped the wire at Cave City again, and spent two weeks listening to official Federal messages. He lived and worked in a thicket two hundred yards from the track, where he had set up his instrument, and sometimes amused himself by sitting near the railroad and watching the trains pass. On his way back, with three or four hundred copies of official Union telegrams—enough to hang anyone—he was discovered and chased by Federal cavalry, eluded them, and returned to Morgan's camp. The telegrams were sent on to General Bragg.

In March, 1863, he was tapping Federal wires close to Gallatin, "near the Tunnel on the Louisville and Nashville RR." In the first twenty-four hours, he took down a message describing an impending movement of Union troops that required immediate action. Starting at five in the afternoon to warn Morgan, he rode all night. About dawn he met a Union cavalryman. There was a pistol fight, and Ellsworth was hit four inches above the ankle. He rode twenty miles with only one foot in the stirrup, till he could get a conveyance to McMinnville, where he could find medical aid.

Morgan let him recuperate till June, then ordered him back to duty for a raid into Ohio. On the way across Kentucky, Morgan detached Captain Ralph Sheldon and Ellsworth, with a small force, to pass around Columbia, Kentucky, and destroy bridges and culverts on the Louisville & Nashville Railroad. Sheldon also hoped to capture a train or two.

As the little force approached Lebanon about 4:00 A.M. on July 4, 1863, they paused to tear up track, went on about five miles to Lebanon Junction, tore up more track, and settled down to wait for the next train. When it did not arrive, Ellsworth cut into the telegraph line as he had the year before, and began calling Z, signing as B, as he had in 1862. The Federals had neglected to change their call letters.

Ellsworth nearly ruined his usefulness because he did not know what messages the real Lebanon Junction operator, E. H. Atwater, had been receiving. He asked why the train was delayed.

"Why," protested Atwater, "you sent a message around by Danville, Lexington, and Louisville this morning, saying a party of Rebels came to within three miles of Lebanon and destroyed the railroad and telegraph and not to let the trains come. And now you ask where they are!"

Ellsworth had to think quickly. "Well," he replied, "that was the report brought in by some drunken section men, who were probably on a Fourth-of-July spree; and, failing to get your office, a message was sent round by Lexington."

After hearing that and perhaps remembering what had happened the year before, Atwater demanded a confirmatory statement from Mr. Knox, the ticket agent at Lexington. Realizing that he could sign Mr. Knox's name as well as any other, Ellsworth tapped back: "My telegram of this morning was based on reports brought in by some drunken men and is without foundation. Let the train proceed."

Ellsworth then amused himself by adding a glowing account of the Fourth of July celebration they were going to have in Lebanon and invited Atwater to come as his guest.

The 8:30 P.M. train from Louisville puffed into Lebanon Junction about this time, and the worried conductor, who had heard that guerrillas were about, asked Atwater for news. The operator reassured him, flashed the news to Ellsworth, added, "the Train is off I must go—" and swung aboard.

Captain Sheldon hastily got his men into position opposite a break in the rails, and waited.

The train came chugging along, pausing a few miles outside the town to take on a guard of Union soldiers. Before it had quite reached the first break in the line, the Confederates flagged it to a halt, because they did not want to wreck the train and hurt people. But the engineer began to slow down too late, struck the break, and derailed part of his train. The train guard opened fire at once, and then the Confederates began firing. There was a lively little fight for about twenty minutes, during which Atwater set off down the track to get help from Lebanon. Almost at once he ran into Ellsworth and two or three other Confederates, who made him prisoner. The two men had, of course, never seen each other.

Ellsworth asked the captive's name.

"Atwater."

"You are the operator at Z," said Ellsworth, "and I was talking with you over the line this morning, having cut the wire and connected this instrument. I found out what I wished and am the one who invited you to Lebanon. I am Ellsworth, George Ellsworth, Morgan's operator."

Atwater, not unreasonably, suggested that Ellsworth, having invited him to Lebanon as a guest and then trapped him, owed him a drink, at least; but before that problem could be settled, Federal cavalry appeared in the distance. Ellsworth and his companions rode for their lives.

Atwater was free. He now had the satisfaction of tapping the line himself and sending General Boyle, in

Louisville, news that Morgan was somewhere near Lebanon.

This seems to have been Ellsworth's last major deception, though he presently had the satisfaction of capturing three Union telegraphers. He himself was captured, however, as were most of Morgan's men, in the advance through Indiana and Ohio. After his release, he took charge of all General Beauregard's telegraphy. By poetic justice, he found Union operators, on two or three occasions, tapping his own wires.

10

The Tennessee Spies

Sam Davis

Though he was operating alone when the Federals captured him, the Tennessee Confederate, Sam Davis, was not always a solitary adventurer. In his earliest recorded exploit, he was one of a trio operating with a larger group of agents on various missions. After his victory over the Federals at Chickamauga, General Bragg knew that more Union troops would certainly be sent against him from Middle Tennessee, Alabama, and perhaps Kentucky, where the Union had its most easily available troops. How many would there be? When and where would they move? Which divisions would be sent against him? Sam Davis, of Capt. Henry B. Shaw's Scouts, was one of several secret agents ordered to find out.

Chickamauga was fought September 19–20, 1863. On September 24, Bragg sent for two of his spies, P. N. Matlock and James Castleman, and personally gave them their orders. They were "to go on scout [i.e., spy] service on the Louisville and Nashville railroad and ascertain the numbers of troops from Bowling Green, Ky., to Nashville."

At the same time, unknown to them for the moment, Sam Davis was being sent into nearly the same area. He had orders to ascertain the strength of Federal units between Nashville and Decatur, Alabama, and he was carrying money for the illicit purchase of U.S. Army pistols.

If these three agents succeeded, Bragg would have full information on all Union troops along a line deep into Kentucky on the north, straight across Middle Tennessee, and south into Alabama. And his soldiers would have a few more pistols—the Confederates were always short of arms.

When Matlock and Castleman returned to quarters from their talk with General Bragg to get ready for their trip, they found they were going to have company. Another secret party of four—Tom Brown, Mose Clift, Elihu Scott, and James Freeman—were also going into the Union lines. Brown was part of Shaw's intelligence group. The others may have come from Carter's Scouts. With the possible exception of Brown, they were not primarily concerned with military intelligence. Their main duty was to bring back recruits for the Confederate Army. Sam Davis was not in the party at all—not yet.

The group went to the home of Meredith Saunders, near Sugg's Creek Camp Ground, within, or nearly within, the Union lines. Here Matlock and Castleman went off on a special mission of their own. When they returned, they found the others had secured fifteen recruits and had been joined by two Confederate officers.

Since the recruiting party was waiting for more men to

come in, Matlock and Castleman took advantage of the delay to visit their families, who lived some miles from Nashville. As they were approaching the Matlock house, they hid their horses in a wood and walked on toward the turnpike. Suddenly they saw someone run across the turnpike. They hailed the mystery man—who turned out to be Sam Davis. As he also had orders taking him to Nashville or its vicinity, Davis proposed they all go together. This would make it easier for the other two to enter the city, because he already knew exactly where the Union pickets were posted.

About nine thirty that night, the trio reached the Matlock home, where they found Mrs. Matlock's brother, Dr. A. P. Grinistead, just back from Nashville with much interesting information. After a late supper and an hour or two of talk, the spies withdrew to sleep in a cedar thicket south of the house—a routine precaution.

Next morning, with six-shooters buckled out of sight under civilian clothing, the three musketeers set out for Nashville, meeting en route a Negro with a two-horse wagon, in which they rode the rest of the way. They knew Union pickets paid little attention to travelers entering Nashville. Getting out again would be the problem.

Taking a room openly at the St. Cloud Hotel, the trio agreed to stay together and fight to the death if detected. After dining at the hotel, they stumbled on a man named Watson, who at once recognized Castleman. Recognition might have been disastrous; but Watson, with sons in the Confederate Army, had no thought of betraying them. Eager to help in any way he could, he agreed to buy pistols from Yankee soldiers, some of whom were willing to make a dishonest penny by trading with the enemy— and the spies were liberally supplied with pennies for just such purposes.

Watson proposed storing these illegal purchases in an outhouse near his home in South Nashville, where they would be safe until the spies picked them up on their way back to Bragg's army. If, in the meantime, the trio were arrested, there would be nothing to identify them as gun-runners. All this was dangerous for Watson, since Nashville civilians had been ordered by the Federal command to surrender all arms. He cut down his risks by storing the pistols outside his house, where they were less likely to be traced to him if discovered.

While waiting for Watson to make his illicit purchases, Davis and his friends, strolling about the city, noticed that many Federal officers tethered their horses outside the courthouse, carelessly leaving their pistols strapped to their saddles. This was something to remember. It would be convenient to have horses when they wanted to leave town; and the Confederates, who could always use more horses, could also use more saddles and more pistols than Watson could buy.

During their stay in Nashville, the three had seen, from a distance, a good many people they knew. So far, except for Watson, they had seen them in time to avoid them, but sooner or later, if they lingered, they were sure to be seen and recognized. It was time for them to leave.

They made some final purchases—new hats, boots, and ten pairs of spurs, other articles that Confederate soldiers badly needed. At dusk they strolled hopefully to the courthouse. Waiting till several officers had tied their horses in the vicinity, they selected the three best, making sure each saddle had two revolvers strapped on, and rode quietly to Watson's house in South Nashville. Here they picked up two sacks filled with Yankee pistols and rode on to safety. After a midnight supper at the Matlock home, they retired to the cedar thicket and checked their loot. Besides the three additional horses, new hats, new boots, new spurs, they had fifty-three pistols—forty-seven from Watson and two from each of the stolen chargers.

Taking one horse, four pairs of spurs, and eight pistols, Sam Davis rode away. His two companions never saw him again. They went on to their own rendezvous with the recruiting party, took their recruits and stolen weapons, and returned to report to General Bragg.

"He thanked us for what we had done," Matlock said.

And well he might! Every moment of their journey had been filled with danger.

Sam Davis reached General Bragg's headquarters safely, perhaps during the last week of September, 1863. A month or so later he was sent out again.

This time Bragg wanted to know what new Union divisions were coming in, when they would arrive, what routes they would follow. Shaw was ordered to find out. It was an urgent mission, as the General's whole tactical plan would depend on what his scouts could learn. They were to send or carry this information from the vicinity of Nashville to Decatur, Alabama, where a secret courier line would pick it up and carry it to Bragg on Missionary Ridge, outside Chattanooga.

The mission was so important that Captain Shaw went in himself, taking a small group, including Sam Davis. These experienced men slipped through the Federal outposts without incident. Probably Shaw was wise enough not to let the whole group move together; he certainly made them scatter when they were inside the Union lines, since they had been assigned to observe different Federal units at separate posts. But they knew how to keep in touch with their leader.

By November 9, 1863, Shaw and his spies had gathered enough information to necessitate another report to General Bragg. This, together with another batch of Northern newspapers, reached Decatur, Alabama, at nine o'clock on the evening of November 10, so that Bragg certainly had the information by November 12.

About this time, a teacher named A. L. Sharp, who had once had Sam Davis as a pupil, chanced to meet him. The young soldier incautiously remarked that he had been detailed as a scout for General Bragg's headquarters. Though that remark was a technical breach of security, there was no great harm in it, since Sam had said nothing about espionage. But it was dangerous for him to add that he was operating in Middle Tennessee. That was equivalent to admitting that he was a Confederate secret agent, as the area was held by Union troops. To make matters worse, Sam remarked, "We have orders to go in again next week," adding that, if he came within fifty miles of his home in Smyrna, he would "make a dash to get there."

The schoolmaster pricked up his ears. His wife was living in or near Smyrna; he gave Sam a letter for her, which Sam's father could forward.

Davis left Bragg's camp on his last mission, November 10, 1863. At the same time, a large detail of agents from another reconnoissance group set out on a very special intelligence mission Bragg had ordered—no one is quite sure what it was.

A further indiscretion on Sam Davis's part had added to his risks. As he approached his target area, he encountered a roving band from the 4th Alabama Cavalry, sent to reconnoiter near the towns of Winchester and Fayetteville, Tennessee, and Athens, Alabama. The local guide promised them had failed to appear because of illness in his family. Local Confederate sympathizers, however, sent word that "a Confederate scout who came in here this evening" would replace him. The new guide was Sam Davis, just arrived from Decatur, the town that served as advance base for Confederate agents entering Tennessee.

Davis rode with the Alabama horsemen all night, reaching Fayetteville in time to breakfast openly at the local hotel. There the group separated. Lieutenant Cal Hyatt took a detail eastward toward Winchester, while Davis and others moved toward Tullahoma, a little farther north, pausing to dine with a Confederate farmer—another of Davis's useful acquaintances. After rejoining Hyatt, they paused again to shoot up some incautious Yankee cavalry. Lieutenant Hyatt and his men then started south toward Huntsville, Alabama, to rejoin their regiment.

Davis, invited to return to safety with them, replied he had still to complete his mission for General Bragg. It was bad enough to admit he was on a special mission, which he should have discussed with no one. But Sam also rashly volunteered the information that he was trying to locate Federal troops in Middle Tennessee, learn their strength, and collect data on fortifications. Captain Shaw's other secret agents, he added, were already at work near Columbia and Pulaski.

No doubt young Davis knew he was talking to trustworthy Confederates; but it was, nevertheless, the kind of remark a man on a highly secret mission ought never make. Had any of these men been captured or talked accidentally to the wrong person, or had any not actually been the genuine Confederate soldiers they seemed to be, Union intelligence officers might have learned everything. A few days later, this same guileless willingness to trust any man in a gray uniform led Sam Davis to his death.

After leaving the cavalry, Sam appeared in the night at the house of Dr. Everand Patterson, some miles from Nashville, where he gave his usual signal, a pebble flung against a window. By this time, it was more dangerous than ever for an agent to stay in a private home, and Sam told Kate Patterson, the doctor's daughter, that he would go on to the Rains Thicket, also called "Rains's Woods," and hide there. This was a wild, densely wooded area of some three hundred acres, half a mile north of Dr. Patterson's house along the Nolensville Pike. On the pike were three houses belonging to various members of the Rains family, hence the name. When spies were concealed in those woods, local sympathizers signaled their approach by a "bob white" whistle.

Sam's lair was not very far from Dr. Patterson's home, for when Kate rode out with breakfast for Sam and feed for his horse, she expected his coffee to keep warm in an earthenware jug. Thirty years afterward, when she told the story, she would say, ". . . and, oh, he did enjoy his good warm breakfast."

He gave Kate a list of purchases to make for him that day in Nashville. She returned with these things about sundown, and that night Sam left to join Shaw.

Captain Shaw decided, about November 18, that another bundle of newspapers and a new report must reach General Bragg at once. There was other important intelligence: General Grant had gone to Chattanooga to take personal command against Bragg. General Sherman's Union troops were moving in the same direction. General Dodge had moved his Union troops from Corinth, Mississippi, to Pulaski, Tennessee. Certainly there was going to be another Union attack on General Bragg. Joshua Brown, one of the scouts, who had seen and counted all the Union artillery and almost every Union regiment, believed they were moving gradually toward Chattanooga.

Sam Davis met Shaw somewhere near Pulaski on Thursday, November 19, 1863. The captain provided him with a fresh horse and handed over the urgent report and other incriminating papers. He also gave him three cakes of soap and three toothbrushes for General Bragg's use. (As it turned out, it was Union General Dodge who made use of them.)

Though he had a cipher, Shaw sent these highly incriminating dispatches in clear. Probably he dared not take time to encipher them, since the information was urgent. At any rate, he took a chance. After all, few of his couriers had been intercepted.

Sam Davis spent either the night before he met Shaw

or the night after at Big Creek, the home of Polk English, another of Coleman's Scouts. He had probably come directly there from the Rains Thicket.

The farm at Big Creek had been a spy rendezvous so long that even the slaves knew what was going on, but all these Negroes were loyal to their masters. The English family's farm was just north of Pulaski, where General Dodge had now placed the headquarters of the left wing of the Union XVI Corps. Here Shaw's men could live in comparative safety near the enemy's headquarters, while two devoted slaves, Houston and Martin, went down into Pulaski, where the agents themselves were too well known to dare appear. The slaves never roused Federal suspicions. Few Northerners had any idea of the devotion of some Southern Negroes to their masters. Yankees assumed that all slaves favored the Yankee cause—which was not at all true.

On the eighteenth or nineteenth of November, Sam Davis took time to observe "the line"—a term that probably referred to the railroad rather than to the Union picket line. Meanwhile, Polk English and the slave Martin went to Pulaski. Boldly approaching Union headquarters, they had the luck to overhear two careless officers discussing Confederate espionage.

About this time General Dodge's monthly report to higher Union headquarters was due, and his military secretary—probably one of the two chatty officers—had left a penciled draft on the office table before the final approved copy was made in ink. In some way, this paper reached Captain Shaw. He said later, after the war, that the papers were stolen from Dodge's table "by a negro boy that once belonged to Mr. Bob English."

The slave delivered the papers at the English farm on Big Creek, saying that they might do "Marse Sam" some good. He was right. They were very valuable papers indeed, for they described the Union forces at Murfreesboro, Shelbyville, and Pulaski.

When Sam Davis set off on November 19, 1863, on what proved to be his last mission, he was carrying these papers and also detailed drawings of the fortifications at Nashville and other Tennessee towns. When Davis began his ride to Bragg's headquarters on that date, Tom Joplin started out with him, but they soon separated, probably for greater safety. That evening, not long after their paths divided, Joplin ran into Federals, had a fight, and was wounded. But he managed to struggle on to Bragg's army.

Young Davis did his best to secrete the dangerous documents he carried. He sewed some of the papers into his saddle. Others he put into his enormous cavalry boots, so big that some troopers carried an extra pistol there. He carried a hank of yarn over his shoulder, with papers tied into it. Inside his haversack he had a ball of yarn, also containing papers.

Before he started out, Sam had been told that a Confederate captain was somewhere in the vicinity, trying to get back to his own lines. The "Confederate" captain was really General Dodge's chief of scouts, Chickasaw, a native of Alabama, but devoted to the Northern cause. His real name was L. A. Naron. Because his home was in Chickasaw County, Alabama, General Sherman had once called him "Chickasaw," and the nickname stuck.

Chickasaw, star of the Dodge intelligence organization, had been living "on the run" in Alabama and Mississippi during the early part of 1863. Having finished that secret mission, he had returned to Dodge's headquarters and was now directing the recently enlarged Union counterintelligence group, then looking for Coleman's spies. Assisting Chickasaw in this assignment was the formidable Sergeant James Hensal, of the 7th Kansas Cavalry, the "Jayhawkers."

Chickasaw's agents had been capturing a series of accurate reports by Confederate spies, one of which was signed by Coleman. They did not know who Coleman was, except that he was head of an enemy spy ring. It was plainly a dangerous ring and General Dodge was much disturbed.

To make matters still worse for Shaw and his men, a Confederate prisoner had escaped a few days earlier. He must have been an important prisoner, since Chickasaw himself had joined in the hunt, and other agents poured into the area in unusual strength. Chickasaw had also sent a special patrol of three disguised Union soldiers on reconnoissance along the Tennessee River. Cavalry swarmed on the roads, for Union General Dodge was moving troops, and these forces also had patrols out. The uniformed patrols were not specially looking for spies, but they were certain to halt and interrogate any unexplained individuals they found wandering about.

Two of Chickasaw's men, Privates Joseph E. Farrar and R. S. King, met Davis on the road about fifteen miles south of Pulaski and stopped him. All three were in Confederate uniform—Chickasaw's men in false uniform, of course. Davis had a Federal overcoat over his true uniform. It had been dyed until it was more or less black, as was not uncommon. Confederates needing clothes often used what they could get from their Union prisoners or from captured Union supplies. Sam, the real Confederate, was not in the least suspicious, supposing that he had met two fellow Confederates, who were merely overzealous about conscription.

Farrar and King were clever enough not to arrest Davis at once; they just pretended to think he was a civilian and insisted on "conscripting" him. They apparently also pretended not to notice the gray uniform under the overcoat.

Sam tried to explain. There was no sense in conscripting him for the Confederate Army, because he was already in it. He had been in it for the last three years, and he was "a true Southern man." To prove it, he then did the worst thing he could possibly have done. He showed his pass, signed "Capt. E. Colman Cmdg Co. of Scouts." Shaw had given him this to get him past Confederate patrols and pickets, and he would have been quite right in showing it—if Farrar and King had really been Confederates. When Farrar refused to honor the pass, poor Davis went a step further and got himself in deeper: he offered to show "something else," probably meaning the dispatches for Confederate General Bragg.

Having by this time seen enough to feel sure of the truth, the two Union men wasted no more breath in questions. They refused to examine any more papers and said they were going to "conscript him by Authority of Col. Cooper for the Confederate Service." (Cooper was Adjutant General in Richmond, in charge of conscription and recruiting.) They took their prisoner at once to

Captain Chickasaw, whose Confederate uniform was enough to convince Sam Davis he was a Confederate.

As it seemed natural for Confederate soldiers to take him to a Confederate officer, poor Sam answered Chickasaw's questions frankly. His captors did not reveal their true identity, and not until they demanded his weapons did he become suspicious. He hesitated before turning them over, saying that he did not believe they were Confederate soldiers; but they were three to one and he had to yield.

When they were within two miles of the Union camp, Davis realized the truth: he was a prisoner in the hands of Federal agents. He tried to escape by spurring his horse, but the scouts were watching and one of them caught his bridle rein. As they rode on toward General Dodge's headquarters, Sam began to get rid of incriminating papers as well as he could. He managed to throw away the skein of yarn he had been carrying on his shoulder and the ball of yarn in his haversack. But when his captors searched his haversack and found incriminating documents there and in his boots and saddle, someone remembered seeing him throw something away. Union soldiers went back and found papers hidden in the yarn. The young man's doom was sealed by the letters to General Bragg's provost marshal and by his Confederate pass. That fatal bit of paper still exists among General Dodge's papers in Des Moines. It looks much as it must have looked when taken from Sam Davis: folded down almost to the size of a postage stamp, worn, crumpled, stained with perspiration and dye from the uniform.

Even a hasty examination of the documents by

General Dodge showed at once that the group of Confederate spies operating locally was alarmingly well informed. What worried the general most was that the Coleman scouts were obviously getting confidential data from someone high in Dodge's own command. He was, therefore, most anxious to identify the mysterious "E. Colman," who was obviously spymaster for Confederate General Bragg in Middle Tennessee and in touch with a highly placed traitor somewhere in Dodge's own command.

When Sam Davis was brought to headquarters, Dodge personally questioned him. He wanted to know where "Colman's" spies were getting so much and such dangerously accurate intelligence. He also wanted to know the routes they were using to penetrate the Federal lines, the names of other spies, and the identify of "Colman." If Davis would give him this information, General Dodge would spare his life. If not, Sam would hang.

The general made this same offer several times at different interviews. Each time, Sam refused; and the general, though secretly admiring the courage of the young prisoner, could only send him back to confinement.

General Dodge did not know it, but at that very moment, Shaw—"Colman"—and one of his best agents, Joshua Brown, were already among the Confederate prisoners at Pulaski, confined in the same prison as Sam. While Chickasaw had been prowling about the countryside, other Federal soldiers had been sent out to find the hidden headquarters of the rebel spies. They found the Schuler house, one of the headquarters of Shaw's spies, and there, or near it, captured "an old, seedy, awkward-looking man in citizen's clothes" who called himself "Dr. Shaw" and said he had once been a Confederate Army surgeon. They took him back to Pulaski and locked him up, never realizing they had captured the much-wanted head of the whole intelligence ring.

Joshua Brown, when captured, had a great deal of important information, but he carried it all in his mind, not in writing. Hence no incriminating papers could be found on him when he was arrested, and he was therefore regarded as an ordinary prisoner, as was Shaw himself. Captured within a few days of each other, Davis, Shaw, and Brown were all sent to the Pulaski jail. They recognized each other instantly, of course, but they took care to give no sign of recognition. Brown escaped a little while later. Shaw remained a prisoner of war for a long time, but the Federals never knew he was the espionage leader they had tried for so long to catch.

Knowing they were safe themselves while still unidentified and painfully aware that nothing they could do would save Sam Davis, Captain Shaw and Joshua Brown waited anxiously in the jail wondering whether Federal pressure could, in the end, persuade him to betray them. Both knew that one word from Sam would hang them in his place; and, though Shaw had confidence in Davis, he became nervous each time he saw him taken away for interrogation. This happened several times, for, besides General Dodge himself, the local provost marshal, the chaplain, and Captain Chickasaw all tried to persuade him to save himself, by revealing the secrets of the spy ring; but the gallant lad steadfastly refused.

The Federals even put one of their own soldiers, disguised as a Confederate prisoner, into the jail as a stool pigeon. He was to make friends with Davis, trick him into admitting to his new friend that he really was a spy, and thus convict him. But to John Randall, of the 66th Illinois, Sam revealed nothing. Randall thought there were other Federal detectives, on errands like his own, put in to associate with Davis. If there were such men, they failed. Sam gave away no secrets.

Once it became clear that Sam Davis could not easily be frightened into talking, the Federal court-martial began. There were two charges against him:

> 1: "Being a Spy," with the specification that he had come "secretly" within the Union lines to gather intelligence. But it was not specified that he was in false uniform.
>
> 2: "Being a carrier of mails communications and information from within the lines of the U.S. Army to persons in arms against the Government." The specification to this charge said that he had been arrested while carrying mail to the rebel army.

Captain Chickasaw was the first witness, then Privates Farrar and King, the two men who had made the capture.

Asked about "the dress of the prisoner when taken," Farrar replied that "he seemed to have been dressed in his own uniform except one of our overcoats dyed black or of a dark cast which he wore." The other replied that "he had on something like a gray suit, dressed in Southern clothes."

Question by the judge advocate: "Did he wear the uniform of the Confederate army?"

Answer: "Yes Sir he did."

At this point, Davis could and should have been acquitted and sent back to the Pulaski jail as an ordinary prisoner of war. He was in his own uniform, and the men who captured him said so. Therefore he was not a spy. He had indeed carried dispatches, but what of it? That was an ordinary military duty. He had carried them within the Federal lines. That, too, was an ordinary military duty. Sam Davis could not be regarded as a spy so long as he was in his own uniform.

It was a very irregular court-martial. To begin with, the defendant had no defense counsel. It is true he had been offered counsel and had declined. But this was a capital case. No prisoner should go on trial for his life without counsel, especially a young and inexperienced boy. The first charge was contradicted by the prosecution's own witnesses. The second charge was not an offense at all. In other words, the court-martial was a series of blunders by volunteer officers very imperfectly acquainted with the rules of land warfare.

The court adjourned the same day to consider its verdict. Next day it found the prisoner guilty on both charges and sentenced him to be hanged on November 27, the day after Thanksgiving.

Everyone concerned was much distressed. The boy's captors, after three years of war, knew how to appreciate bravery and devotion to a cause. General Dodge was particularly impressed by his prisoner, dark-haired, standing six feet, "a fine, soldierly-looking young fellow, not over twenty." Sam was again offered not only his life but freedom—if he would give information.

When Sam still refused, the Union Army regretfully

prepared to hang him. Some Pulaski ladies were allowed to visit him. So were the local Methodist minister and Chaplain James Young, 88th Ohio. To the latter, the boy at the last moment gave his dyed Federal coat. The chaplain kept it for several years after the war, then sent it back to Tennessee. It is still cherished in the War Memorial Building in Nashville.

Toward the end, Sam was kept handcuffed. Joshua Brown remembered how young Davis was brought into a room where other prisoners were eating. Without a sign of recognition, Brown handed him a piece of meat. Unable to handle a knife and fork in handcuffs, Davis lifted it with both hands.

They took him from the jail with arms pinioned, placed him in a cart, and seated him on his coffin. From the jail window, Shaw and Brown watched the dismal little procession. Davis's arms may have been freed or loosened after he had mounted the death cart, for Brown said later that Davis saw his two friends and saluted as he passed. The guards led the death cart slowly out of town. A Union drummer boy beat the dead march. The doors and windows of Pulaski houses were closed. One woman lay on her bed with a pillow over her head to shut out the dreadful slow throb of the drum. She would never know how much that Northern drummer boy was to admire and respect—all his life long—the young Southern soldier he was escorting to the gallows.

Upon arriving at the scaffold, Davis asked the Union officer in charge how long he had to wait.

"Just fifteen minutes. I am sorry to be compelled to perform this painful duty."

"It does not hurt me; I am innocent; I am prepared to die and do not think hard of you."

He was interested in the latest news from Bragg's army and remarked, "The boys will have to fight the rest of the battles without me."

He had to endure a final, dreadful—and obviously deliberately planned—test of his endurance. A soldier heard an officer at the gallows say, "Mr. Davis, you have but five minutes to live unless you give up your secret." Sam refused three times. At the last moment, Captain Chickasaw galloped up. It might have been a reprieve—but it wasn't. Chickasaw merely brought a last chance to accept General Dodge's offer. Sam could still save his life; he knew how. A Union soldier, standing nearby, heard the conversation.

"Do you suppose that I would betray a friend?" asked Sam Davis. "No, sir; I will die a thousand times first. I will not betray the confidence of my informer."

Chickasaw told Davis he was not the man who ought to be hanged, "and if you would yet tell me," he added, "who General Bragg's chief of scouts was, so that I might capture him, your life would yet be spared."

Sam, who knew that the man Chickasaw wanted was at that moment a prisoner in the Pulaski jail, looked his tempter in the eye: "Do you suppose, were I your friend, that I would betray you?"

Then Chickasaw reminded the condemned boy that life was "sweet to all men."

Davis said he was not that kind of man. "You may hang me a thousand times and I would not betray my friends."

There was nothing more to say and only one thing to do. They adjusted the noose. At the last moment, Davis stood very straight and pushed his hair back. It was the last second.

Someone said that he fell three feet and thirty inches. No pain, no struggle. He died at once.

"I wish that man could have gotten away," said a Union soldier as he marched away from the scene. Many others felt the same way. They knew the chance for life that Davis had been offered and were filled with respect for his courage.

The drummer boy in blue who sounded the dead march for the execution was a mere lad named L. W. Forgrave. He remembered the horror of the hanging all his life, and Sam Davis's supreme courage. He used to tell his sons about it, drumming the beat on the arm of his chair as he talked.

Chickasaw felt about the same way: "Thus ended the life of Samuel Davis, one of General Bragg's scouts," he reported, "a noble, brave young man, who possessed principle. I have often regretted the fate of this young man, who could brave such a death, when his life rested in his own hands. His mind was one of principle."

A Union soldier wrote in his diary, ". . . he stood it like a man. . . . he never paled a bit but stood it like a hero."

Sometime later, a fellow prisoner came upon Captain Shaw, who looked at him with eyes filled with tears. Shaw handed him the paper he had been reading, a copy of the *Pulaski Citizen*.

It contained the story of the execution of Sam Davis.

Dee Jobe

DeWitt Smith Jobe, known among his Confederate Army friends as "Dee," was the second member of Coleman's Scouts who chose to die rather than betray secret information. Some time in the late summer of 1864, he entered the Federal lines with Tom Joplin and a few others. Their orders were to examine the little towns of College Grove, Triune, and Nolensville along the Nolensville Pike, which led north to Nashville. Jobe was on familiar terrain, since his home was in Triune.

The group had agreed among themselves that, in case of imminent danger, they would scatter and continue operations separately, working as far apart as possible. Each man would thus have a better chance of getting back with the intelligence General Bragg needed.

Danger of some sort must have threatened on August 29, 1864, for Jobe rode alone all that night to reach the home of William Moss. This house was set back from the turnpike about two hundred yards, between Nolensville and Triune. Moss, who had two sons in the army, gave him breakfast. Afterward, Jobe hid on a neighboring farm, pausing at the farmhouse to see a girl from Triune named Betty Haynes. It has always been a legend in the vicinity that Jobe secured a good deal of information from a local girl, and Betty Haynes may have been his source.

Somehow the Federals learned that a Confederate agent was somewhere in the vicinity. Fifteen mounted infantry from the 115th Ohio, commanded by Sergeant Taylor E. Temple, arrived from Murfreesboro and, when they found no one, began to search. They examined the entire countryside with a large telescope and saw a horseman riding past a cornfield on a neighboring hill. They investigated.

Following the hoof marks, Temple's patrol soon caught up with Dee Jobe, who had just time to chew up the papers he was carrying before the Federals seized him. He was then only about six miles from his home.

Then followed one of the most horrifying episodes of the Civil War. It was plain that Jobe had military information. When he refused to reveal it, the Union troops tried torture. Like Sam Davis, Dee Jobe stood firm.

But not for Dee Jobe was the relatively easy death of the gallows. His captors began by demanding what had been in the papers he had destroyed. Jobe refused to say. They threatened to kill him. He still refused. They beat him over the head, knocked out his front teeth—and still learned nothing. Then they put a leather strap around his neck and dragged him over the ground until they either strangled him or broke his neck. The yells of the torturers could be heard a mile away.

After this act of savagery, the Union soldiers belatedly felt admiration for Jobe's courage. He was, some of them said, the bravest man they had ever seen. But they left his body lying by the road, where a young woman, a friend of the Jobe family found it. She spread a handkerchief over the face, and it was probably she who notified Jobe's family. "Old Frank," a slave who had nursed the young soldier in childhood, brought the body home and dug a grave.

The dead man's cousin, DeWitt Smith, of the 45th Tennessee, left his regiment at Chattanooga, and returned home to avenge Jobe's death. He began near Tullahoma. Here he entered a camp of sleeping Union cavalry, stole a butcher knife, and entered two tents, each of which contained eight men, killing every one. As Smith was cutting the fifteenth throat, the last man stirred in his sleep and sat up. Smith fled.

So, at least, declares Tennessee tradition. It seems doubtful that so much slaughter was possible in complete silence, though similar feats were managed by the Indians.

Smith could rely on co-operation from Rutherford County people, furious over the torture of Jobe. He once forced two Yankee prisoners to go with him to a farmhouse, where he molded bullets while the housewife cooked a meal for him, then marched his captives about half a mile, shot them both, dropped their bodies in a sinkhole, and left the message: "Part of the debt for my murdered friend, Dee Jobe."

11

Tragedy in Arkansas: David O. Dodd

The tragedy of Sam Davis in Tennessee had an almost exact parallel in the fate of the equally brave David O. Dodd in Arkansas. Both were captured in Union terrain with incriminating data on Union forces; both were carrying papers that indicated expert intelligence work somewhere; both were hardly more than boys; both were asked for the names of those working with them; both refused to give them; both were offered their lives for betrayal; both refused that, too—and both were hanged. Two Union officers later contributed to a monument for Davis; at least one Union officer to a monument for Dodd. Even the names of the places where they were executed were the same: Davis was executed at Pulaski, Tennessee; Dodd in Pulaski County, Arkansas.

However, there were differences in the two cases. Davis was a soldier, Dodd a civilian. Davis was an experienced secret agent, Dodd an amateur on his first mission. Davis, being in uniform, ought not to have been regarded as a spy; Dodd, being in civilian clothes, certainly was a spy.

Young Dodd came of a Texan family that had moved

to Benton, Saline County, Arkansas, near Little Rock, which is in Pulaski County, where the father had established business interests while his son was still a child. The boy had been a student at St. John's Masonic College in Little Rock, but about the time the war began, he left to study telegraphy. He was soon employed in the Little Rock telegraph office and, later, after the Union Army entered the city, began clerking in Union sutlers' stores, the post exchanges of the day. When his family went south, he worked in the telegraph office in Monroe, Louisiana. The elder Dodd decided that someone ought to return to Little Rock to look after the family property, and he sent David, thinking that his son's youth would enable him to get into the city, now occupied by the Federals, without difficulty.

This purely business trip would have presented no problems if young Dodd had not been induced by someone to collect military information. He needed a pass to move through the area the Confederates still held. General James A. Fagan, local commander, provided one. Dodd said later that the general refused to issue it, except in return for espionage. The Confederates wanted to know the Federal positions, strength, and plans— "plans" may have meant war plans or maps. When arrested, Dodd was carrying full details on Union artillery and brigade organization. Since no officer would expect a youngster without training to collect this kind of intelligence unassisted, it is clear that David Dodd had been told to make contact with one or more agents in Little Rock.

Young Dodd rode into Little Rock with another Confederate spy just before Christmas, 1863, about a month after Sam Davis had been hanged. The second agent was Frank Tomlinson, nearly the same age as Dodd, from the town of Pine Bluff. The two had no difficulty passing Federal guards on their way in, but they separated when they reached the city.

Tomlinson, whose mission was to collect intelligence, either by his own efforts or with the aid of resident agents, got his information quickly but in some way roused suspicion. With Federal troops chasing him, he escaped across the river into what is now North Little Rock. Here he found refuge in the house of a farmer, who dressed him in girl's clothes, including a sunbonnet to hide his face, and set him to work. When his pursuers arrived, they searched the house, but they paid no attention to the young girl busily occupied with ordinary household chores. When they had gone, Tomlinson went quietly on his way to report to the Confederates.

David Dodd at first aroused no suspicion in Little Rock. He was an agreeable youth—"an unusually handsome and manly, though extremely modest little fellow," said a girl who knew him. He stayed at his aunt's home as if on an ordinary family visit and moved about freely for some time.

During the Christmas holidays he lived the normal life of mid-nineteenth-century youth, dancing and seeing a good deal of three girls: Mary Dodge, supposed to have given him information; Mary Swindle, who went to a dance with him; and Minerva Cogburn, to whom he had brought letters from his sister. Some Little Rock girls were almost certainly getting information from Federal Army officers, and all three of these may have been gathering it for Dodd.

Mary Dodge is supposed to have been the girl who gave David the information later found in Morse code in his notebook. Her own father, Dr. R. L. Dodge, thought she had been dabbling in espionage and was afraid the Federals would find it out. When David Dodd was arrested, the doctor packed his daughter off to relatives in Vermont as fast as he could. Mary was not told what had happened to her friend David until long afterward.

The memorandum book Dodd carried contained the notes on the strength and positions of the Union forces that the Confederates had asked him to get. But he had naïvely written his information down in the Morse telegraphic alphabet—as if nobody else could read Morse—and that was bound to attract attention. Any telegrapher could read those dots and dashes. Dodd's notebook is now filed with the court-martial documents in the National Archives in Washington. With it are two braided locks of long hair David was carrying, probably keepsakes from both Marys. He had also been foolish enough to keep his pass from Colonel Crawford, commanding the Confederate outposts. He had with him both Federal and Confederate money, and "two letters from Rebels of this city [Little Rock] to parties outside our lines." However, he had been careful to leave his loaded derringer pocket pistol at his uncle's house, on Upper Hot Springs Road, before entering Little Rock.

When he left the city, Dodd rode a mule past one sentry without question, but was halted by a Federal picket about eight miles on the road toward Hot Springs. Questioned, he said he was going fifteen miles into the country to see friends and that he would be traveling on the Hot Springs road. The picket, Daniel Olderbury of

Company E, 1st Missouri, told Dodd that he would not need the pass any more, and he, as a guard, would keep it. Olderbury did keep the pass until he was relieved; then he tore it up.

Beyond this point, young Dodd was outside the Federal lines and apparently safe. He jogged along on his mule till he reached his uncle's house, where he got his pistol. Then he started back to Little Rock, but turned off on a crossroad that would take him to the Benton road. He was only a mile or two now from the picket post at which he had given up his pass.

At the point where the crossroad joined the Benton road, he ran into another picket and was halted. Asked by the Federals for his pass, he explained that the picket on the Hot Springs road had already taken it. Asked where he lived, he replied, "Little Rock."

Where was he going?

"To a man's by the name of Davis."

Where was he going from there?

"Down on some creek to get him a horse."

The sergeant knew someone higher up would have to handle this mysterious traveler. He sent Dodd to regimental headquarters.

Here First Lieutenant C. F. Stopral demanded either a pass or some other identification. Dodd had a general pass from a Federal post at Princeton, Arkansas, which was addressed to all pickets and scouts, but he did not hand it over. Instead, he handed over the memorandum book, which contained his notes in Morse. The lieutenant knew enough telegraphy to spell out some of the Morse alphabet. What he read was more than suspicious: "The 3rd Ohio battery has four guns. Braes 11th Ohio Battery has six guns." There was more information about Federal artillery.

Why was a young civilian carrying this around?

The lieutenant took Dodd to his captain, George Hanna, 1st Missouri cavalry, who also had a post on the Benton road.

The prisoner Dodd again explained that his pass had been taken from him at the picket line on the way out. The captain asked if he could recognize the man who took it. When Dodd said he could, the captain sent him out to the picket line under guard. But the guard had been changed. Instead of examining the roster to find the right man, they simply sent Dodd to the guardhouse.

When he was searched there, he was found to have Confederate money, Confederate postage stamps, the loaded derringer pistol, and concealed letters. One letter was Minerva Cogburn's reply to his sister. The letters contained no military information, they were ordinary friendly correspondence.

The prisoner was sent back to the provost marshal. Captain Robert Clowry, Assistant Superintendent of the U.S. Military Telegraph (later President of Western Union), was called in. Under his expert scrutiny, Dodd's notes in Morse proved to be even more incriminating than the Federals had at first suspected, with much detailed information on Federal cavalry and infantry brigades. This was espionage. No doubt about it.

As with Sam Davis in Tennessee, there were efforts by local civilians to save Dodd when he was found guilty and sentenced to hang. And as with Davis, the general in local command, General Frederick Steele, offered Dodd his life if he would reveal the identity of his informants.

This would have involved Mary Dodge and probably several other people. Dodd replied, "General, I can die, but I cannot betray confidence."

They hanged him January 8, 1864, on the campus of St. John's Masonic College, where he had once studied. Mary Swindle, who had been with him at a dance the night before he was captured, saw him taken past her father's house on his way to the gallows. Like Davis, Dodd was given one last chance to save himself as he stood on the scaffold, but he said, "I have no disclosures to make; hurry up your execution."

An inexperienced hangman bungled matters badly. When there was no cloth with which to bandage the boy's eyes, he told his executioner, "You will find a handkerchief in my coat." Then the rope was too long, so that Dodd fell with his feet touching the ground and soldiers had to haul up the rope hastily to let him drop again.

His grave in the Mount Holly Cemetery, Little Rock, is still an Arkansas shrine. Part of the inscription is in Morse code.

12

Spying in the Wilderness

Early in the morning of May 4, 1864, General U. S. Grant began his advance toward the terrible Battle of the Wilderness, which was followed by equally terrible conflicts at Spottsylvania (May 7–20) and Cold Harbor (May 31–June 12), months of siege warfare at Richmond and Petersburg—and then Appomattox and the end.

Grant's advance through the Wilderness was no surprise to General Robert E. Lee, for his spies had been telling him for weeks exactly what was coming. They had, indeed, been keeping the Confederate commander so completely informed that even his own officers wondered at the exactness of his information.

When the fighting in the Wilderness was over, Captain Charles Minor Blackford wrote his wife: "How General Lee finds out Grant's intention I cannot imagine, but, as soon as Grant commenced to move, Lee commenced also, though, in some instances, as much as twenty miles apart; yet when Grant formed his new line, there was Lee in front of him as surely as if they had moved by concerted action."

None of Lee's officers (except the chosen few who shared the secret) could guess how their commander did it, either. All they knew was that Lee had an uncanny way of discovering exactly where Grant was going—and getting there first.

In fact, it was this perfection of Lee's espionage that enabled him to hold off Grant's superior army so long. His forces were so small that his only hope was to concentrate at exactly the right spot at exactly the right time. It was hard enough to hold off the Army of the Potomac at best. If Lee ever concentrated at the wrong spot, he would never get another chance.

Except that it was a main part of their duty to keep silent, two groups of men and women could have explained the mystery to Captain Blackford and other curious officers. One was the group of secret agents and couriers operating the Confederate intelligence network in Washington and the North. The other was a specially chosen group of Confederate scouts and spies operating at the front, along enemy lines and deep within them, penetrating Grant's lines, observing enemy positions, watching every troop movement, and reporting it all to Stuart or to Lee.

But the information that came in from the first group of distant spies in Washington and all over the North was mainly "strategic" intelligence. That is, it dealt with the far-reaching general plans of the Northern leaders, the strength of their armies, the positions they held, their commanders, their supplies, their morale—all the general information needed long before the shooting starts. Intelligence of this kind had to be supplemented by "tactical" intelligence, that is, the kind of information needed when the shooting does start: where a particular regiment is going, what position it holds, what its commander can do, how high morale is, and things like that. Such last-minute tactical information has to be gathered by experienced scouts and secret agents, sent out by local commanders in the field, moving continually in the enemy's front and rear, even inside the enemy's camp—desperately dangerous work.

Stringfellow and Mosby were such men—scouts, spies, and front-line fighters. Of equal value to the Confederates was Channing M. Smith, of Company H ("the Black Horse"), 4th Virginia Cavalry, which was also Stringfellow's regiment. Working with them were others of equal skill and courage: Sergeant "Ike" Curtis, Sergeant Dick Hogan, Sergeant George D. Shadburne, Hugh H. Scott, though less is known about them.

Channing M. Smith had his own way of doing things. Though he practically lived with the Union Army, he disliked entering the enemy's lines alone and usually took along his "regular guide," a certain M. B. Chewning, though he had other assistants when Chewning was on other duty.

Chewning was Smith's companion on one particularly gratifying occasion. The two spies' suspicions had been roused when they saw three Federal cavalry horses tethered in front of a country house. Their hopes also were roused when, as they approached, they saw three Union soldiers emerge from the house carrying large baskets.

Taken by surprise and handicapped by their burdens, the Yankee trio were easily captured and compelled to carry the baskets to a safe and secluded spot. Here, in comfort, under an oak tree by a small stream, at a safe distance from the enemy, Smith and Chewning examined their loot. They were delighted to find a large pan of hot baked potatoes, hot white rolls, cold tongue, strawberry jelly, cheese, and a bottle of whiskey. There was even silverware and a drinking cup! All this luxury had been meant for Union officers who would never enjoy it now.

Another ever-faithful spy was Colonel John Mosby, still engaged in independent reconnoissance of his own. Mosby made the Federals so much trouble that some Union men thought the mere effort to track him down was in itself enough to delay General Grant's advance. This Southern guerrilla and spy was so capable that he won the Northern commander's sincere admiration. After the war, when General Grant became President of the United States, he did everything in his power to help the officer who had caused him so much trouble during the war. He even secured responsible Federal government jobs for him.

Long before Grant's troops began to move, Confederate spies in the North began to send warnings to both General Lee and Jefferson Davis. One remarkable and very early report on General Grant's exact intentions was dated March 24, 1864—more than five weeks before the Army of the Potomac began to move. It was one of the most valuable bits of intelligence the Confederates had secured since Mrs. Greenhow's early successes. It told not only what Grant was going to do, but also—with almost mathematical exactness—how many troops he would have to do it with.

Unfortunately, after all the risks the spies had run to

get it, the report did the Confederates no good at all. Union detectives intercepted it on April 12, when they arrested Miss Sallie Pollock. Sallie, only seventeen, had been running an intelligence center in Cumberland, Maryland, where she received by mail the reports of Confederate spies, then carried them south. She had long been making secret journeys down the Shenandoah Valley to Staunton, Virginia, fording the Potomac River on horseback, flirting with any Union pickets she happened to meet, and finding shelter in the homes of relatives along the way. She had come under suspicion earlier, and had been arrested twice, but had always talked herself out of trouble. This was the first time the Federals had been able to catch her with incriminating evidence.

Union detectives found her carrying two copies of the same letter, one for General Robert E. Lee, one for Confederate President Jefferson Davis. The fact that, though these were dated March 24, Sallie still had them three weeks later shows that the Confederate secret couriers had been slow and cautious. They had probably been having a difficult time working their way southward through the Northern states without being caught. But even though the transmission of this all-important news about General Grant's intended move and the size of his army was slow, these letters—if they had ever been delivered—would have warned the Confederates a month or more in advance, with surprising accuracy, what was going to happen.

Confederate spies kept the Northern Army of the Potomac under careful observation all through the winter of 1863-64, with plenty of help from civilian sympathizers within the Union lines. One winter night Shadburne and some of his men roused an unidentified Confederate girl sympathizer at Fairfax Court House, which had been occupied by the Federals for years. She guided them through the darkness to a house three miles away, where they secured information on a Federal force at not-too-distant Centreville and on the movement of Federal trains. This girl was probably Antonia Ford. Antonia had been spying for Mosby and other Confederates, like Shadburne, until she was finally arrested in March, 1863.

The spies also maintained a continuous watch over the Orange & Alexandria Railroad, which ran southwest from the vicinity of Washington through the country where the coming battles would be fought. Movement of Federal troops and supplies along this line was essential information for the Confederate leaders. A count of passenger cars would show how many troops were passing. A count of freight cars would give some idea of Union supplies.

Channing Smith, some time in that early spring, rode through Union General Meade's artillery park, then went on to the headquarters of V Corps, where he sat for some time with his hand on the staff of the headquarters flag, hoping for a chance (which never came) to pull it down and make off with it. But on this same reconnoissance, he went to General Meade's own headquarters, where he did contrive to steal a small flag, which he triumphantly presented to General Lee.

Most of this midwinter reconnoissance and espionage amounted to little more than keeping the Yankees under observation and making sure there were no sudden moves that might take the Confederate Army by surprise. But by April, or a little earlier, various spies were reporting signs that the Union Army would soon be on the move. Shadburne reported that the whole Army of the Potomac had been paid on Tuesday, March 1; also that Kilpatrick's Federal cavalry had returned, in early April, from raiding Richmond, and then set off on another march, carrying three days' rations; and that the Federal command had sent its sutlers to the rear. Then on April 10, Smith was able to confirm Shadburne's report with additional facts. Not only had the Federal command sent sutlers, traders, and other nonmilitary personnel to the rear, it had ordered all baggage back to Washington. Clearly the Federals were contemplating a large forward movement. And that meant a battle.

Two other Confederate agents, deep within the Union lines, were also reporting in early April. These men cannot be absolutely identified; they were probably Stringfellow and Mosby.

On April 10, General Stuart addressed a note "To Capt. Stringfellow, war-path," in which he said, "I have just heard, through Col. Mosby, that the enemy is carrying troops every night from Culpeper towards Alexandria. You must find out the truth."

Stringfellow probably went at once to Alexandria, where he had many sources of information and where he had already carried out numerous espionage missions. Alexandria was the home of his future wife, and he knew many of the people. He had noted that all white troops had been withdrawn from trenches around the town and sent to the Army of the Potomac, their places being taken by Negro troops.

About this time, Stringfellow's secret service very nearly cost him his life. Dressed in a pair of Union officer's trousers, a Confederate gray jacket, and a Union overcoat—thus presenting the outward appearance of a Union soldier so long as he kept his overcoat buttoned— he was leading a small band of Confederate raiders, hoping to capture Federal dispatches and pick up a few prisoners.

While his men were under cover some distance behind him, Stringfellow captured a Federal courier, who, seeing the Confederate spy's blue overcoat, had expected no trouble until it was too late. Calling one of his men, Stringfellow sent him to the rear with the prisoner—and also with orders to bring up the whole detachment. Unfortunately, the guard paused to "go through that Yank" in the hope of finding some loot. He was so engrossed with searching the prisoner that he failed to start Stringfellow's horsemen forward promptly.

While anxiously waiting, Stringfellow encountered two more Union cavalrymen, soon reinforced by a third and a fourth. They had seen him halt the Union courier and were naturally suspicious. Approaching quietly, all four suddenly surrounded him and covered him with their pistols. One of Stringfellow's companions, who was hidden a little to the rear, heard the dialogue that took place and later wrote it down.

"What does all this mean?" demanded Stringfellow, with a convincing show of indignation. "Are you bush-whackers?"

"No, sir."

"If you are not bushwhackers or guerrillas, why do you

capture a United States soldier in his own lines? You must know me. Do you not belong to General Gregg's cavalry?"

"Yes, we do."

"Well, don't you remember seeing me at headquarters?"

So persuasive was Stringfellow's tone that three Yankees promptly did "remember" seeing him there. They could have been right, too, Stringfellow was quite bold enough to penetrate a hostile divisional headquarters. When the sergeant swore he had never seen him, at headquarters or anywhere else, Stringfellow himself assumed an air of appropriate skepticism.

"Boys, it is very easy for you to deny being bushwhackers; it is easy for you to get into our lines with our uniform coats on, but let me see your pants."

Thus far, no uniform had been visible on any of the soldiers except blue overcoats and high cavalry boots. The genuine Union men threw back the skirts of their overcoats and displayed regulation trousers.

"Now," they said, "let us see yours."

This was just what the spy had been hoping for. Carefully keeping his gray jacket covered, he revealed U.S. Army trousers plus the stripe of a commissioned officer. The Yankees stared at it; Stringfellow's tone became very authoritative indeed.

"You see you have insulted an officer."

The three privates wanted to let him go, but the sergeant was still wary.

"There is something wrong about him," he insisted.

Expecting to hear his own cavalry arriving at any

moment, Stringfellow struck a bold note: "Come right on with me to headquarters and I will have satisfaction before I am done with you."

He turned resolutely toward the Union outposts, refusing to give up his arms, waited for a good chance, then suddenly announced he was a Southern soldier, demanded surrender, and began firing. The Yankees' bullets missed. Stringfellow's second shot hit the sergeant, his own men came to his aid at last, a hesitant force of Yankees appeared, and there was a lively skirmish, the wounded Yankee sergeant taking a shot at Stringfellow whenever he had the chance. Eventually, the Confederates fell back, carrying the wounded Yankee sergeant with them. Regretting he had had to wound the man, Stringfellow paid his prisoner's expenses at a Richmond hotel.

Stringfellow had had a similar escape the year before, when his superb knowledge of the Union Army had enabled him to talk his way out of impending arrest. At that time, he met a Federal cavalry detachment which demanded his surrender. He was wearing a Federal overcoat over a gray uniform.

"Surrender?" exclaimed the spy. "What do you mean?"

"We mean that you are a guerrilla and you are our prisoner," said the Yankees.

Stringfellow explained that he belonged to the 1st New Jersey.

"Who is in command?"

"Major Janaway."

"Right. Who commands the brigade?"

"Colonel Taylor."

"Right again. Where is it stationed?"

"In the edge of Warrenton."

"Yes—and who commands the division?"

As usual, Stringfellow knew the right moment at which to assume a tone of irritation.

"My friend, I am tired of your questions. The First New Jersey is in Taylor's Brigade, Gregg's Division, and Pleasanton commands the whole."

"He's all right, boys, let him go."

The Confederate spy rode peacefully forward on whatever mission concerned him at the moment. But one can understand why he told John Esten Cooke, the novelist, then on Stuart's staff, that he never went out on an espionage mission without expecting it to be his last.

In late March and early April, 1864, while occupied in all-important Confederate espionage before the Federal advance into the Wilderness, Stringfellow and Channing Smith were exposed to needless danger by an egregious piece of folly of which General Stuart and Governor William Smith, of Virginia, were equally guilty. Stuart foolishly told the governor about the two spies' under-cover exploits, a matter of the highest secrecy. Governor Smith, careless of security requirements, allowed some of their adventures to reach the newspapers!

When General Lee heard of the leak, he was suf-ficiently alarmed to rebuke Stuart: "I consider the lives of Stringfellow and Channing Smith and others greatly jeopardized. . . . You had better recall them and replace them by others." But the general's final suggestion was not practical, for nobody could possibly replace these two men. Smith and Stringfellow simply had to accept the extra risk. By pure good luck, the incredible blunder of the general and the governor did no harm.

By the last week of March, 1864, alarming news was reaching General Lee. Captain Conrad, Stuart's chaplain spy, had again been feeling around for information in Washington itself. Lee wanted him to learn just where the Union forces were, where they were planning to move, how strong the forces were in men and artillery, and who their commanding officers were. Mosby's prowlings in search for information took him within a mile of Centreville, Virginia, at a time when some of General Burnside's Union troops were passing through the town. Mosby's horsemen picked up a few of them as prisoners. These men assured him that the Union IX Corps had left no troops in Annapolis except convalescents. In other words, the whole corps was on the move. This news went on at once to Lee, who telegraphed it to President Davis on April 30.

Stringfellow had also supplied confirmation on April 28, the very day when General Lee was anxiously inquiring of Longstreet as to General Burnside's whereabouts.

This information was probably rather late in reaching army headquarters, but that was no fault of Stringfellow's. The trouble was, some staff officer, through whom the message came, was careless enough to give the name of the spy responsible for the report as "Franklin." That made a good deal of difference when the telegram reached General Jeb Stuart. If the report came from Stringfellow, he felt it would be as reliable as military intelligence can ever be. If it came from some unknown individual named Franklin, it would have to be given a very low rating indeed. Reliance could be placed only on intelligence from known, and trusted spies, who had earned their reputation for being correct. There was no secret agent called Franklin in the service, but Stringfellow's full name was Benjamin Franklin Stringfellow, though he was never known by that name.

From Fredericksburg, the message was telegraphed to Stuart that "one of your scouts Franklin just from Md [Maryland] near Washington" was reporting that Burnside with twenty-three thousand Northern troops, seven thousand of whom were Negroes, had marched through Washington on the twenty-fifth and had passed near Alexandria. The report was especially valuable because it also confirmed at last the fact that XI and XII Corps, about which Lee had been much disturbed, had not been sent to Virginia at all.

Stuart realized at once that this report was Stringfellow's and therefore reliable. In forwarding it to Lee, he added an unsigned note:

Gen'l
This must be Stringfellow.

13

Secrets of Gettysburg

Neither the Union nor the Confederate Army, as the Gettysburg campaign opened, had much cause for pride in its intelligence service. Union scouts and spies inexcusably failed to notice that Confederate strength on the Rappahannock front had suddenly been reduced from three corps to one. Not for several days did the Federals wake up to the fact that Robert E. Lee and the two missing Confederate Army corps were marching swiftly around the Federals' flank and would soon be in their rear, ready to assail Washington itself.

If the Federals had had this information in time, General Joseph Hooker could easily have let loose the whole Army of the Potomac on the weak one-third of the Confederate Army left by Lee to deceive him. He could then have turned west with overwhelming superiority to crush the other two-thirds. But thanks to a total failure of Federal intelligence, General Lee was far up the Shenandoah Valley, and his II Corps was attacking the surprised General Robert H. Milroy at Winchester, throwing that grieved and astonished man entirely out of town, before the Federals realized where Lee really was.

In this advance, Lee had one special advantage: the Confederates had recently broken the latest Union cipher and had been reading secret Federal messages.

Confederate collection of secret information preparatory to Lee's advance was delayed by one ludicrous bit of misfortune. A secret courier named William Croft Hyslop arrived in Richmond with a cipher message. Like most Confederate ciphers, it could be read only when one had the key word. This was a new cipher with a new key word and, to ensure complete secrecy, the key word had been trusted to no one save the courier himself. But Hyslop, with a good deal on his mind during his dangerous secret journey, had completely forgotten the all-important word when he finally reached Richmond.

Much annoyed, the disgusted authorities in Richmond locked him up in Castle Thunder, where he had nothing to do but think. Finally he managed to remember the magic word! His message, when deciphered at last, was found to come from Confederate sympathizers in Baltimore, reporting that they had two hundred armed men ready to join the Confederates on their northward march, if Lee would only bring his army near the city. The forgetful Hyslop was not employed again as a courier but was put to smuggling drugs for Confederate hospitals. His odd blunder did no real harm, as Lee never approached Baltimore, anyhow.

After the Federals had located Lee and his moving army—when it was almost too late—Union spies began doing excellent work. One particularly brilliant agent,

John C. Babcock, kept the advancing Southern Army under continual observation, moving with it as it approached the Potomac, crossing the river, and moving on through Maryland into Pennsylvania. Other scouts and agents now began to report as the soldiers in gray drew nearer, until at last a steady stream of intelligence was flowing into General Hooker's headquarters. But that was only after two magnificent chances at swift and easy victory had been lost for lack of timely intelligence.

The Confederate intelligence service during the whole Gettysburg campaign was nearly as bad as the Union service had been when the campaign began. Clumsily phrased, ambiguous orders from Lee's headquarters sent General Jeb Stuart dashing so far east of the main body of Confederates that he could get no couriers with news back to Lee. For several critical days immediately before the battle, Lee had no information about the Federals at all.

Not until the Confederate spy James Harrison, working for General Longstreet, arrived from Washington on June 28, 1863, only three days before the battle began, did Robert E. Lee at last find out that the whole Federal Army was on the move. By that time, his own forces were widely scattered over Central Pennsylvania, from Chambersburg to Harrisburg, while the whole Army of the Potomac, with General Meade as its new commander, was concentrating in his rear.

Harrison was a very important spy. He saved Robert E. Lee from a crushing defeat that would have ended the Civil War in 1863 instead of two years later. Lee's forces were scattered over Pennsylvania while the Union Army was closing in behind him. When he received Harrison's news, he regrouped his forces at once and was ready to fight the Federals at Gettysburg—not in time to win, but in time to avoid complete destruction.

Considering how important his news was, it is surprising that for a hundred years after the Civil War, no one could find out who Harrison was. Even his full name was unknown—he was simply "Harrison." But it *was* known that he had appeared in a performance of Shakespeare's *Othello* at a theater in Richmond. One of the authors of this book searched the records of the Richmond stage and proved that the spy was a rather well-known Shakespearean actor named James Harrison. As an actor he was in the newspapers a good deal before the Civil War. He had certainly done a great deal more spying than his Gettysburg adventure. But not a word of his secret service ever escaped him, amid all the publicity. He died in 1913—without a word about his espionage in his obituary, which reported only his theatrical career.

Thanks to Harrison, Lee was able to gather all his troops to fight at Gettysburg, though Stuart did not arrive till the battle was half over. That four-day battle turned out to be one of the greatest in all history—one that war colleges here and abroad have studied ever since.

General Lee was hoping to break the line of the Pennsylvania Railroad, thereby cutting off Federal supplies. He also hoped to raid Harrisburg, Philadelphia, and Baltimore. He did not succeed, though one of his scouts was caught locating a ford over the Susquehanna River at Harrisburg on July 2, 1863, while the battle was at its height. When Pickett's brave and pathetic charge failed on the last day, all hope was gone.

14

The End of the Struggle

The heartbreaking, bloody war in which Americans confronted Americans came to an end when at last, in 1865, General Robert E. Lee surrendered to General Grant at Appomattox.

No Confederate spies seem to have been under death sentence in Federal prisons at the time of the surrender, but one spy, who had had an incredible escape the year before, was now a prisoner for the second time.

This was Private (later the Reverend) J. T. Mann, a practically indestructible Confederate, who had been wounded in the hand and neck at Gaines's Mills, June 27, 1862; had had his hip and thigh broken at Gettysburg a year later; and had then survived a wholly illegal hanging by a mob of Federal soldiers, April 4, 1864. In spite of all this, he was back with the Confederate Army, fighting until he was captured, unhurt for once, in the attack on Federal Fort Stedman, near Petersburg, in 1865. This time, being an ordinary prisoner of war, he was merely jailed and was released after the war ended, on May 28, 1865.

Soon after being wounded at Gettysburg, Mann had been promoted to captain, assigned to espionage, and provided with a forged proclamation offering fifty dollars for his own arrest as a deserter. He was expected to display this, if any Union soldiers showed signs of doubting he really was a deserter. He was also given an expired furlough, likewise forged, which he was supposed to have overstayed—more proof that he was a Confederate deserter. Thus equipped, he was told to go into the U.S. Navy Yard at Pensacola and into Fort Pickens to collect any available information. He entered the Federal lines near Fort Barrancas, opposite Fort Pickens, on the coast southwest of Pensacola, and there became friendly with a sergeant in Company B, 7th Vermont Volunteers.

Mann was soon able to report to General D. H. Maury, Confederate commander on the Gulf Coast, that a U.S. Army paymaster would visit Fort Barrancas, carrying enough cash to pay "all troops in New Orleans and on the Mississippi River and the men in the gunboat fleets." Since the Confederate Army was always short of funds, Maury prepared to seize that cash as fast as possible. Mann was told that a force of Confederates would approach Fort Barrancas and would signal its readiness to attack the fort with a single pistol shot. When he heard the shot, Mann was to set fire to the powder magazine.

On the night of the proposed raid, Mann was up late drinking with his friend, the Vermont sergeant. During the evening he secretly turned his friend's watch ahead by nearly two hours. When Mann left the sergeant's tent about eleven o'clock, the unsuspecting Yankee thought it was nearly one in the morning. Apparently, the Confederate spy had made sure the sergeant had had plenty to drink.

Mann had already provided himself with a ball of twine steeped in turpentine. Almost at once he heard a pistol shot, approached the magazine, lighted the ball, and tossed it toward the magazine—then saw a Union sentry not fifteen feet away. The soldier snatched up the flaming ball and tossed it back at Mann, fired, and missed him. There was no sign of the Confederate attack Maury had promised. The general had canceled it without informing his spy, and someone else had fired a pistol—not an unusual sound around a fort in time of war.

Mann fled, found shelter in the house of a devoted Confederate for three days, and tried to escape on the fourth night but was captured and taken back to the fort. An infuriated mob of Union soldiers, who knew most of them would have been blown to bits if Mann's plan had succeeded, seized him and prepared to hang him without waiting for a court-martial. Throwing a rope over a projecting beam, they hauled him up before anyone noticed that his feet were only an inch or two off the ground, so that he was giving himself a little support with his toes. To prevent that, the mob at once dug a hole in the earth under their victim and then stood about to watch him die. Mann's neck had not been broken by the drop, but he was slowly strangling to death.

At the last moment, his Vermont friend intervened. The soldiers cut their victim down and resuscitated him.

Mann was court-martialed by the Federals but acquitted of trying to destroy the magazine, because the sentry swore (correctly) that he had seen him throw his fireball at 11:30 P.M. The Vermont sergeant swore (incorrectly but sincerely) that he and the spy had been drinking together till nearly one in the morning. No one seems to have realized that Mann was a Confederate soldier in disguise. He returned to the Confederate Army, only to be captured again, though this time as an ordinary prisoner of war. He seems to have been the last Confederate spy to risk death on the gallows.

Other spies were active to the very end. The capture of their leader and the deaths of men like Jobe and Davis did not dampen the ardor of Coleman's Scouts. Shaw, or "E. Colman," was exchanged for a Union prisoner February 16, 1865, and Sergeant Richard B. Anderson saw him at General Joseph Wheeler's headquarters in Georgia on April 9, 1865, the day of Lee's surrender; but General Joseph E. Johnston did not surrender until April 26, and Alexander Gregg, one of Shaw's best agents, and his spies remained grimly at work during these weeks. When General Bragg gave up his command and there was no more need of Confederate espionage in Tennessee, they operated for Johnston around General Sherman's army, and "all the way from Dalton to Atlanta, Johnston knew Sherman's every plan." Said the veteran Sergeant Anderson, "When old Joe Johnston laid down his sword, I was still on old Sherman's rear counting his regiments and his artillery."

Even now at the end of the war, Mosby and his men were not quite ready to give up the lost cause. A few days after Appomattox, Robert E. Lee, worn out and disheartened, went out for one of those night walks that he loved to take through the Richmond streets. He paused at the house of General R. H. Chilton. Though it was com-

pletely dark, he knocked at the door, probably thinking
—in that time of privation—that the family was saving
its candles, as in fact they were. When the Chiltons saw
that their caller was Lee, they brought him in and
extravagantly lit a candle. Channing Smith was standing
before him.

The war was over—just over. And on that April
evening, one of the greatest generals of all time stood in
the house of his friend in Richmond, facing one of the
scouts who had for years risked so much to bring him
intelligence during the war. Smith had just come as a
messenger from Mosby, who was still at large, still in
command of his rangers, still full of fight, and still loyal
to their lost cause.

It had been no trouble—merely like old times—for
Channing Smith to work his way secretly into a Richmond now held by Yankees, with a message for General
Lee. He had been slipping through the Yankee lines for
several years. But the brave scout's eyes filled with tears
as he beheld his general, "now pale and wan with the
sorrow of blighted hopes."

Mosby had sent Channing Smith to ask for orders.
Ought Mosby and his men fight on? They were quite
capable of doing it. Or must they surrender, too?

"Give my regards to Colonel Mosby," said Lee, the
ever-scrupulous, "and tell him that I am under parole
and cannot for that reason give him any advice."

Since his general could not give an order, Channing
Smith asked for personal advice. "But, General, what
must I do?"

"Channing," said his old commander-in-chief, "go
home, all you boys who fought along with me, and help
build up the shattered fortunes of our old state."

Index

JOHN BAKELESS has been a reporter, lecturer, soldier, editor, and college professor, as well as author. Born in Carlisle Barracks, Pennsylvania, he attended the Carlisle Indian School with American Indian classmates. He was graduated from Williams College and received M.A. and Ph.D. degrees from Harvard University. He shares with Ralph Waldo Emerson the honor of receiving Harvard's Bowdoin Prize in two successive years. Since his first book was published in 1921, Mr. Bakeless has contributed to such magazines as *Atlantic Monthly* and *Saturday Review*. His earlier books include *Turncoats, Traitors and Heroes* and *Spies of the Confederacy*, the book for adults on which this version for younger readers is based.

Mr. Bakeless served as a military intelligence officer in the United States Army and has a long-standing interest in the history and methods of intelligence work. His research on the spies of the Confederacy included examination of unpublished documents in archives as far away as Iowa.

KATHERINE BAKELESS is an author, teacher, and pianist. She has collaborated with her husband on earlier books, including *Spies of the Revolution*, and has helped him on others by working on notes, criticizing scripts, typing, and indexing. She has also written two books for young readers on her own, *Story-Lives of Great Composers* and *Story-Lives of American Composers*.